The War Manual

What every true believer in Jesus Christ
needs to know in order to become fully
equipped for the "Real War"

Bill Niland

PRESS

Copyright © 2004 by Bill Niland
Real Deliverance Ministry
P.O. Box 2042
Tarpon Springs, FL 34688-2042

The War Manual
by Bill Niland

Printed in the United States of America

ISBN 1-594673-09-8

Unless otherwise indicated, Bible quotations are taken from the New American Standard Bible. Copyright © 1960, 1962, 1963, 1968, 1971, 1973, 1975, 1977, 1995 by the Lockman Foundation, La Habra, Calif. All rights reserved.

Other Scripture quotations are taken from the New International Version Bible. Copyright © 1960, 1962, 1963, 1968, 1971, 1973, 1975, 1977, 1995 by the Lockman Foundation, La Habra, Calif. All rights reserved.

"For our struggle is not against flesh and blood, but against the rulers, against the powers, against the world forces of this darkness, against the spiritual forces of wickedness in the heavenly places."

Ephesians 6:12

The War Manual

❧ ◆ ❧

CONTENTS

Acknowledgments

In September of 1986, God called me to the ministry of spiritual warfare after turning over my life to him. He had allowed me to experience much of the evils of the occult and selfish living prior to my calling. This was to prepare me to experience the reality of the demonic realm, and to have a first-hand understanding of the enemy. He had told me that my calling was to become my passion. He wants me to equip His people for victory, since the Church is neglecting this vital teaching. Many write books of this nature, but few have experienced both sides of the war in such explicit details.

The subject in this book is very controversial, and yet not new. God has shown and taught me many principles and truths in His word in all my years of serving Him in this calling. This book is to glorify Him alone. Jesus Christ is the Deliverer and Sovereign Ruling Power to be acknowledged first.

I also wish to acknowledge my wife Janet, who has stood by me since day one. She is an anchor in my life, and has also had to put up with the persecution that we receive by being on the front lines of God's army. We come under direct demonic attack—as well as attacks from believers used by demons.

I also wish to acknowledge Pastor Tom Buck of Riverside Fellowship in New Port Richey, FL, for his belief in me and for his support of my calling. He has been an asset to my own spiritual growth and balance. His friendship and wisdom are very important to me, and also to the ministry.

I need to acknowledge a dear old friend of mine. His name is Jim Moody. Jim was the first person who discipled me in the truth of God when I first became saved. He gave me the basic knowledge I needed for understanding about this spiritual war. He taught me who I was in Christ.

I wish to thank Michelle Swedberg of Mountaintop Design for her countless hours and support of the ministry. Her ability to assist in the editing of my written words and grammar is outstanding. Michelle is also the one who designed the ministry's awesome web site: www.realdeliverance.com.

Finally, I wish to thank the many people whose brief portions of testimonies are included at the beginning of each chapter. They are portions of real letters this ministry receives daily. Their names have been omitted for their privacy. They are included to give you a taste of the reality of the war and the enemy's lies.

My hope and desire for this book is to honor my Lord and Savior, Jesus Christ...that it will bless and equip His people, and set the captives free.

Foreword

There are people along one's journey with the Lord Jesus Christ that you thank God for bringing them into your life. Bill Niland is one of those people for me.

In the church today there is either no talk about spiritual warfare or a complete obsession with it in a way that doesn't bring glory and honor to our Lord and Savior. Bill is a breath of fresh air, of one who is pursuing truth and deliverance for anyone who wants it solely for the glory of God. As long as I have known Bill, he has truly been a student of God's Word first and foremost and has a passion for seeing people delivered from the hand of the enemy. God brought Bill and I together and has helped both of us better understand our position in Christ as bondservants and soldiers for God's Kingdom.

In this manual, Bill has clearly outlined the reality of spiritual warfare and has made the battle the Lord's and not the believer's. We are in a battle, but not one that we stand alone to fight. We stand in the strength and the armor of the LORD. Bill has done a great job to show us the tactics of the enemy and how believers allow the enemy and his army to infiltrate their life. This manual clearly outlays the reality of the battle and the necessity for dependence upon the power of the Holy Spirit and obedience to our Lord Jesus Christ.

You will find many books that deal with spiritual warfare, and most of them will be full of not only Scripture but also human reasoning and psychology. This is not so with Bill. Here you will find solely the Word of God as the only tool necessary to bring victory to the life of anyone who will call upon the name of the Lord Jesus Christ. You will find Scripture clearly illustrating the great truths that Bill puts forth for your understanding. This is not a book based exclusively upon experience and speculation but plumbing the depths of God's Word. When Christ came into direct conflict with the enemy, it was the Word of God that He used to cause him to flee. That is why this manual is only a supplement to the true weapon God has given you. This book is not your instrument for victory, but will clearly guide you to use the instrument God has already provided: God's Holy Word.

It is time that our churches quit walking around in defeat and powerlessness and pick up their pieces of spiritual armor and walk in the victory already afforded them in Christ. If you want to find victory and get busy serving a righteous and holy God, then this is the manual for you.

Pastor Tom Buck
Riverside Fellowship Church
New Port Richey, Florida

∾ Chapter 1 ≂

◆

About The War

"Yesterday, I thought to myself within the course of the deliverance, 'I just can't break through.' It was like a fight I never have experienced before, and will never experience again. It has made me realize just how severe sin can be. Satan and the demonic world will do anything to hold us back and oppress us. It all started with a little anger and continued to progress into a big mess."

℧here is an on-going cosmic war between God's kingdom and Satan's defeated kingdom. You are in this war whether you realize it or not, and whether you want to be or not. Since you are in it, you need to be equipped for victory. The Bible says that this war we are in **is not against your fellow man, but against demons**:

> **Ephesians 6:12** *For our struggle is not against **flesh and blood**, but against the **rulers**, against the **powers**, against the **world forces** of this darkness, against the **spiritual forces** of **wickedness** in the**heavenly** places.*

Let's look at the Greek words and definitions from the Strong's Lexicon in regards to Ephesians 6:12. Your understanding of these terms is vital to being able to grasp the concepts in this book. Even though this section may seem a little "technical," it will help you in the long run:

Flesh 4561—sarx—probably from the base of 4563; flesh (as stripped of the skin), i.e. (strictly) the meat of an animal (as food), or (by extension) the body (as opposed to the soul (or spirit), or as the symbol of what is external, or as the means of kindred), or (by implication) human nature (with its frailties (physically or morally) and passions), or (specially), **a human being** (as such):–carnal(-ly, + -ly minded), flesh(-ly).

Blood 129—haima ("hah'-ee-mah")—of uncertain derivation; **blood, literally (of men** or animals), figuratively (the juice of grapes) or specially (the atoning blood of Christ); by implication, bloodshed, also **kindred:–blood.**

Rulers 746—arche ("ar-khay'")—from 756; (properly abstract) a commencement, or (concretely) **chief (in various applications of order, time, place, or rank)**:–beginning, corner, (at the, the) first (estate), magistrate, power, principality, principle, rule.

Powers 1849—exousia ("ex-oo-see'-ah")—from 1832 (in the sense of ability); privilege, i.e. (subjectively) **force**, capacity, competency, freedom, or (objectively) **mastery** (concretely, magistrate, **superhuman**, potentate, token of control), delegated **influence**:–authority, jurisdiction, liberty, power, right, **strength**.

World 165—aion ("ahee-ohn'")—from the same as 104; properly, an age; by extension, perpetuity (also past); by implication, the world; specially (Jewish) a Messianic period (present or future):– age, course, **eternal**, (for) ever(-more), (n-)ever, (beginning of the, while the) world (began, without end). Compare 5550.

Forces 2888—("kos-mok-rat'-ore")—from 2889 and 2902; a word ruler, an **epithet of Satan**;-ruler.

Spiritual Forces 4152—("pnyoo-mat kos'")—from 4151; non carnal, ie.(humanly) ethereal (as opposed to gross), or **(demoniacally) a spirit** (concr), or (divinely) **supernatural**, regenerate, religious;-spiritual. comp 5591

Wickedness 4189—poneria ("pon-ay-ree'-ah")—from 4190; **depravity**, i.e. (specially), malice; plural (concretely) plots, sins:– iniquity, **wickedness**.

Heavenly 3770—ouranios ("oo-ran'-ee-os")—from 3772; celestial, i.e. **belonging to or coming from the sky**:–heavenly.

From the definitions above we can see the definite difference between those involved in this war. This is a vital truth to grasp. The reason this is vital is because it gets your eyes and mind on a bigger picture than what you perceive is going on around you.

You see, when people hurt you or attack you, the tendency is to focus the anger, hurt, and pain against the person. However, as you read this manual you will learn that actually, people are used by demons—as victims and casualties of war—to hurt and victimize you. This allows you to have forgiveness and compassion on those who hurt, abuse, molest, and attack you. If you have unforgiveness toward anyone, you are not struggling with the one you should be: *the demons!*

The Two Sides

God's Kingdom consists of its citizens and His holy angels. The citizens are those who have put their faith and trust in the finished work of Jesus Christ and have become a believer.

> **1 Timothy 5:21** *I solemnly charge you in the presence of God and of Christ Jesus and of <u>His chosen angels</u>, to maintain these principles without bias, doing nothing in a spirit of partiality.*

> **Philippians 3:20** *For our citizenship is in heaven, from which also we eagerly wait for a Savior, the Lord Jesus Christ;*

> **Ephesians 2:19** *So then you are no longer strangers and aliens, but you are fellow citizens with the saints, and are of God's household,*

Satan's kingdom consists of himself, his angels (or more commonly known as demons), and those who reject Jesus Christ in this world.

> **Revelation 12:7** *And there was war in heaven, Michael and his angels waging war with the dragon. <u>The dragon and his angels</u> waged war,*

> **1 John 3:8a** <u>*the one who practices sin is of the devil;*</u> *for the devil has sinned from the beginning.*

> **John 8:44** <u>*You are of your father the devil, and you want to do the desires of your father.*</u> *He was a murderer from the beginning, and does not stand in the truth because there is no truth in him. Whenever he speaks a lie, he speaks from his own nature, for he is a liar and the father of lies.*

Satan and his demons have already captured the unbelievers in the world system. So the real battle is between the children of God on one side, and Satan and his demons on the other. This war is raged both against individuals and corporately against the church. Satan's army has been opposed to God and His creation since the dawn of mankind.

> **Revelation 12:17** *So the dragon was enraged with the woman, and went off to make war with the rest of her children, who keep the commandments of God and hold to the testimony of Jesus.*

Jesus came to destroy the works of Satan.

> **1 John 3:8b** *The Son of God appeared for this purpose, to destroy the works of the devil.*

<u>Jesus has already defeated Satan and his demons at the cross and stripped them of all power over the believer.</u> However, they are still here until the end of the age, and the believer must stand against them in the power of Christ in order to have the victory. It's similar to the situation an occupying army faces after winning a war: they know they have won, but they must still be on guard against disgruntled opponents. If they don't, they may end up with a bullet through their chest.

> **Colossians 2:15** *When He had disarmed the rulers and authorities, He made a public display of them, having triumphed over them through Him.*

The Satanic army's main purpose is to cause the believer to live a defeated Christian life and thereby rob God of His glory. They seek to render the believer useless to do the will of the Lord, and even to enslave the believer to do the will of Satan.

> **2 Timothy 2:25–26** *with gentleness correcting those who are in opposition, if perhaps God may grant them repentance leading to the knowledge of the truth, and they may come to their senses and **escape from the snare of the devil, having been held captive by him to do his will.***

In order to stand victoriously in this cosmic war, the believer needs to have an abiding relationship with the Lord. However, the believer also needs to understand many other principles in order to stand. Almost all believers go out into the battlefield without using the weapons of armor God gave them upon salvation. At the top of the list of things needed is knowledge.

God said, in Hosea 4:6, *"My people are destroyed for a lack of knowledge."*

With the knowledge contained in God's Word, the believer will learn that he is fully equipped for battle. The power of God is in us, and works through us, as shown here in Ephesians:

> **Ephesians 1:19–22** *and his incomparably great power for us who believe. That power is like the working of his mighty strength, which he exerted in Christ when he raised him from the dead and seated him at his right hand in the heavenly realms, far above all rule and authority, power and dominion, and every title that can be given, not only in the present age but also in the one to come. And God placed all things under his feet and appointed him to be head over everything for the church,* (NIV)

Here is some of the essential knowledge that can be gained from God's Word:

- Knowing who you (as a believer) are in Christ.
- Understanding about the renewing of the mind.
- Understanding how to use the weapons of warfare that God has already given to you.

Unfortunately, most churches today have already been deceived by doctrines of demons.

> **1 Timothy 4:1** *"But the Spirit explicitly says that in later times some will fall away from the faith, paying attention to deceitful spirits and doctrines of demons"*

They teach believers that this cosmic war was only in old Biblical times and is not relevant for today. I am sorry if you are reading this and you have been led astray by adopting that belief.

This false teaching gives Satan's army an advantage over the deceived believer. Many believers go down without a fight and with an overwhelming sense of hopelessness. They are destroyed for a lack of Biblical knowledge and are fed false knowledge, or lies, from the enemy instead. Many are even taught not to concern themselves with demons. Satan's army can—and will—easily capture ignorant believers who do not submit to God.

The truth is, Satan has no power over a believer except what is given to him by the believer (Romans 6:13 & 16) When you do not understand—or utilize—your Christ-given authority, you give up that authority to Satan. The issue of giving up power to Satan will be discussed in Chapter 6.

On the other hand, Satan and his army are fearful of a fully armed, fully equipped, knowledgeable believer who submits to God and stands in the authority of Christ. This type of believer knows how to overcome and defeat the enemy and send them retreating. The fully-equipped believer is able to recognize the attacks or schemes of the enemy.

> **2 Corinthians 2:11** *"so that no advantage would be taken of us by Satan, for we are not ignorant of his schemes."*

The fully-equipped believer walks in faith, power, and victory. You will learn how and why by studying this manual.

You may already be enslaved to demonic forces or know someone who is. If you would like to know how to stand and live a victorious Christian life, then this *War Manual* is for you. You will be exposed to God's truth and knowledge, and realize what has been missing in your Christian life. Spiritual warfare is part of the Christian life.

The truth will set you free!

Chapter 2

❖

Can a Christian Be Demonized?

"My friend attends church and is very much saved. She loves the Lord. Those at her church don't think that demons can possibly indwell a believer. She is a Christian and very suicidal. She is receiving secular help (a self-mutilator support group). She has lost her job because of her problems and labeled with Bi-polar disorder right now. She has been hospitalized in the past and is afraid she will be again and lose her child."

B efore we begin the study, I feel it is necessary to clear up a word used in Christian circles. Many use the word, or have this idea of, demon *"possession"* - which was translated into most Bibles as such. "Possession" implies ownership and total control. God is the only One who owns or "possesses" anything. He alone is Sovereign.

The correct translation of the word in its original meaning *"daimonizomai"* [1] or its equivalent *"daimonizomenos"* is our word, *"demonized"* – a word that is used in the Bible every time to describe the condition of those controlled by, or under the dominion of, a demon spirit or spirits. Hopefully this will help you to understand more deeply as we look at the subject of spiritual warfare and its relationship to the believer in Christ.

Have you ever stopped to wonder why the body of Christ is weak and defeated today? Many believers are sick in the body (not all sickness is demonic), emotionally hurting, carrying unforgiveness, depressed, or feeling guilt and condemnation about their past. Many feel insecure and inadequate with a low self-image, are held captive to addictions of alcohol, nicotine, drugs, or pornography, are driven by lusts and perversion, and are just plain defeated in life.

This oppression of Christians can be the work of Satan. Satan can accomplish this work through demonic spirits operating in the lives of believers who do not abide in Christ, thus making a provision in the flesh.

Some Signs of a Demonized Person

Before we answer this question of Christians having demons, it might be helpful to discuss what "having demons" looks like.

Please note: Not all of these signs have to be present for someone to be considered demonized. Conversely, the presence of *some* of these signs does not necessarily mean the person is in fact demonized. However, if any of these signs and/or other sins (which are not listed here) are a recurring pattern in a person's life, I would suspect that this person has a demonic stronghold.

These are just some of the common signs of a demonized person. They are listed here as a reference: [2]

- A compulsive desire to curse the Father, the Lord Jesus Christ, or the Holy Spirit.
- A revulsion toward the Bible, including a compulsion to deface or destroy the Bible.
- Strong suicidal or compulsive violent thoughts.
- Deep-seated, irrational feelings of intense bitterness and hatred toward individuals or groups (e.g., ethnic groups).
- Any compulsive temptation that forces you to think or act in a way you truly do not want to think or act.
- Compulsive desires to destroy the reputations of, attack the character of, and lie about other people; using vicious and cutting remarks to injure those perceived as a threat to a problem area of your life.
- Terrifying, persistent, and overwhelming feelings of guilt and worthlessness even following sincere confession to the Lord of known sins.
- Physical symptoms that appear suddenly and pass quickly for which there is no medical or other basis; these might include choking sensations, pains that move around the body, feelings of tightness around the head and eyes, dizziness, blackouts, or fainting seizures.
- Deep, persistent despondency and depression.
- Recurring dreams and nightmares that are especially horrifying and disturbing, or clairvoyant dreams of things that later take place.
- Sudden, unprovoked surges of violent rage, uncontrollable anger, or seething hostility.
- Debilitating and persistent doubt regarding one's salvation.

More serious demonic activity

- Inability to live normally
- An expressed or exhibiting kinship with death and the dead.
- A proneness to violence; exhibiting unusual strength when violent.
- Severe behavior and personality problems

- Persistent restlessness, agitation, and insomnia.
- A sense of intense inner anguish and torment.
- Self-inflicted injuries (i.e., cutting, burning, etc.) or recurrent injurious accidents.

Who is Deliverance For: Unbelievers or Believers?

This is an important question since many Christians have believed the lie that Christians (believers) cannot be demonized.

Who is a Believer?

Since there are so many promises given to those who are believers, it is very important to establish exactly whom the Bible classifies as a believer. The Greek word for "believe" is "*pist-yoo'-o.*" [3] It indicates one relying on Jesus Christ the Lord and His finished work on the cross for his or her salvation. So anyone who puts his faith and trust in *Jesus Christ alone* for salvation is a real believer.

Who is an Unbeliever?

An unbeliever is anyone who rejects Jesus Christ the Lord—and Him *alone*—for his or her salvation. This includes people who believe that they must contribute to their salvation (because that is not accepting Him *alone*). Some examples are those who follow religions and cults, or those who rely on themselves. In a nutshell, the Bible classifies them all as sinners.

The term "deliverance" can be defined as "being set free from the molestation of the enemy." Deliverance can only be for believers who have allowed themselves to be molested and captured by the enemy. The fact is that *only* a believer can stay free from demonization—by living a life submitted to God and walking by the Spirit.

> **Galatians 5:16** *But I say, walk by the Spirit, and you will not carry out the desire of the flesh.*

Since a believer has the Holy Spirit in him, he is free from the power of sin.

> **Romans 6:18** *and having been freed from sin, you became slaves of righteousness.*

> **Romans 8:2** *For the law of the Spirit of life in Christ Jesus has set you free from the law of sin and of death.*

However, an unbeliever is not free from the power of sin. Even the so-called "good things" they do is still sin.

> **Isaiah 64:6** *All of us have become like one who is unclean, and all our righteous acts are like filthy rags; we all shrivel up like a leaf, and like the wind our sins sweep us away.* (NIV)

> **John 15:5** *I am the vine;* **you** *are the branches. If a man remains in* **me** *and I in him, he will bear much fruit;* **apart from me you can do nothing***.*

Unbelievers belong to Satan and carry out his will. They are used by him and his demons.

> **John 8:44** *You are of your father the devil, and you want to do the desires of your father. He was a murderer from the beginning, and does not stand in the truth because there is no truth in him. Whenever he speaks a lie, he speaks from his own nature, for he is a liar and the father of lies.*

If demons were cast out of unbelievers, they would only be let back in again. The unbeliever *cannot* walk according to the Word of God. He does not have freedom from sin without Christ, nor the power and ability to submit to God without the Holy Spirit (Colossians 1:11 and 2 Timothy 1:7). The conclusion is that deliverance is for believers only.

But How Can a Christian Be Demonized?

The Bible warns believers not to give the devil opportunity in your life.

Ephesians 4:27 *and do not give the devil an opportunity.*

Opportunity occurs when you make a provision in your flesh through sin and disobedience. This may be either willfully or out of ignorance.

Romans 13:14 *But put on the Lord Jesus Christ, and make no provision for the flesh in regard to its lusts.*

When you make provision in your flesh and obey its lusts, you are enslaving yourself to Satan's kingdom. <u>The Bible says we become a slave to the one we obey</u>.

Romans 6:13 *and do not go on presenting the members of your body to sin as instruments of unrighteousness; but present yourselves to God as those alive from the dead, and your members as instruments of righteousness to God.*

Romans 6:16 *Do you not know that **when you present yourselves to someone as slaves for obedience, you are slaves of the one whom you obey**, either of sin resulting in death, or of obedience resulting in righteousness?*

You are called to be a slave or a bondservant to Christ!

Ephesians 6:6 *not by way of eye service, as men-pleasers, but as **slaves of Christ**, doing the will of God from the heart.*

A bondservant is someone who offers himself for service and slavery by choice, as opposed to a forced slavery. We must see the difference between choosing to serve and *choosing to be a servant*. When we chose to serve, we are still in charge. We decide whom we will serve and when we will serve. And if we are in charge, we will worry a great deal about anyone stepping on us; that is, taking charge over us.

But when we choose to be a servant, we give up the right to be in charge. There is great freedom in this. If we voluntarily choose to be taken advantage of, then we cannot be manipulated. When we choose to be a servant, we surrender the right to decide when we will serve. Paul wrote of himself as a bondservant.

> **Titus 1:1** *Paul, a bond-servant of God and an apostle of Jesus Christ, for the faith of those chosen of God and the knowledge of the truth which is according to godliness,*

Fortunately, when a believer does give a place for the enemy to operate in their life, God has also provided the way for deliverance by repentance. We will look at this more in Chapter 13.

When you are in the ministry of casting out demons, you are always challenged by a certain question: "Is it possible for a born-again believer to be demonized?"

"Absolutely no way!" many will exclaim, "The Holy Spirit cannot coexist in the same body of one who is demonized!" If that statement is true, then how can the Holy Spirit dwell in a body that has sin? Do you have sin in your life even though you have received the Holy Spirit?

Yet I repeatedly counsel with and cast demons out of (by the power of Christ) born-again believers who really love God with all their hearts. Most Christians have wrongly reasoned that they could not be demonized because the Holy Spirit is in them. This is logic from man and false doctrines of demons...and not from God. The issue is an understanding of the flesh. The Bible is clear that there is <u>NO GOOD</u> thing in the flesh.

> **Romans 7:18** *For I know that **nothing good dwells in me, that is, in my flesh**; for the willing is present in me, but the doing of the good is not.*

This includes the Holy Spirit, who is good and perfect. He does not reside in the flesh, which is sinful. The flesh is but a tent or housing for our spirit. The spirit part of the believer was regenerated and born again. This is where the Holy Spirit resides. When this flesh or body dies, it cannot inherit the Kingdom of God since it is corrupted. Our spirit is what goes to be with the Lord.

The flesh was circumcised from the spirit. It was cut away when you became born again.

> **Colossians 2:11** *and in Him you were also circumcised with a circumcision made without hands, in the removal of the body of the flesh by the circumcision of Christ;*

The Holy Spirit does not dwell with sin, nor does He dwell with demons. The Holy Spirit does not even dwell in the flesh. The flesh was circumcised from the spirit; it is not as one with the spirit man, but separate. God is able to dwell in His Holy Temple that He made.

> **1 Corinthians 6:19** *Or do you not know that your body is a temple of the Holy Spirit who is in you, whom you have from God, and that you are not your own?*

Paul is not saying that the body is holy, but that within this body of flesh is the Holy Temple, and this body or flesh should be in submission to Him. The flesh is sinful and corrupt. It does not desire to submit to God, but rather to sin. The flesh can be offered up to sin and disobedience, and in turn, offered up to demons. This is how one can become demonized as a believer.

Remember, the word used is "demonized," and its meaning is "to be under the control of, or dominion of, demonic spirits." Whether you wish to believe this dominating control is from within or from without is your choice. **Regardless, it is not worth arguing about.** The way to freedom is still the same in either case: *repent and submit to God.*

However, I can say to you that I believe the demonic control is from within. I base this belief on the Scriptures dealing with the flesh, as well as on my years of experience. Through God working in me, I counsel and deliver believers who are held captive by demons. Many of these believers manifest demons through voice and action. A demon would have to be inside to be able to control one's bodily functions. Of course, demons can (and do) also

29

harass and molest believers from the outside, too. We can always be attacked or buffeted in this war.

According to the Scriptures, demons do leave your soul and body when you become born again. The spirit man is changed and you are then made complete in Christ.

> **Colossians 2:10** *and in Him **you have been made complete**, and He is the head over all rule and authority;*

However, if the new believer is not discipled in the things of God and in knowing his new nature in Christ, demons can, and do, move back into that believer's life as spiritual squatters:

> **Matthew 12:43–45** *Now when the unclean spirit goes out of a man, it passes through waterless places, seeking rest, and does not find it. Then it says, 'I will return to my house from which I came'; and when it comes, it finds it unoccupied, swept, and put in order. Then it goes, and takes along with it seven other spirits more wicked than itself, and they go in and live there; and the last state of that man becomes worse than the first. That is the way it will also be with this evil generation.*

This happens when a new believer chooses to walk in *continual* sin and disobedience (out of ignorance or of his own will).

Salvation is the freedom from the curse of death and punishment; at salvation we also receive the power or ability through Jesus Christ to have victory over sin and the molestation of the enemy. We are to be overcomers (see Rev. 2 & 3) as well as to be conformed to the image of Christ. Jesus cast out the physical wrongdoers from the Old Testament temple; we must also cast out all the spiritual wrongdoers (demons) from the temples of our lives!

Jesus has delivered your *spirit* man from the power of Satan. But you must stand and resist the molestation or harassment by the enemies until you (with His power) have freed both your soul and body. This is why we were given weapons of warfare.

A Christian can be harassed, tormented, afflicted, and demonized in an area of his or her life and still be a very sincere Christian. Demonization can vary from a mild harassment to extreme bondage, where the body and mind become dominated and held in slavery by demons—which is a demonic stronghold.

What are Some Results of Denying that a Christian Can Be Demonized?

When it is denied that believers can be demonized, then unscriptural teachings (which are really false doctrines of demons) are proclaimed as truth (1 Timothy 4:1-2). These false teachings have become associated with some of the following problems that engulf the church today:

1) People are left open to be trapped into cults, false religions, and vain imaginations.

2) All inherited characteristics and personality quirks are thought to be unchangeable, with no hope of being free of them.

3) Mental health programs teach that all problems are the result of heredity or chemical imbalances, and try to treat everything with a pill.

4) Demons torment the victim in secret.

5) An inability to forgive others and be free of bondages and addictions.

6) Anyone who walks in faith and power, and who does what Jesus commanded us to do, is looked at as being crazy or glorifying demons and Satan.

7) The fear of demons is fostered and promoted by Satan and his demons.

8) Believers are left with living a defeated Christian life.

The following verse was written to the early Christian church:

> **2 Timothy 2:25–26** *"Those who oppose him he must gently instruct, in the hope that God will grant them repentance leading them to knowledge of the truth, and **that they will come to their senses and escape from the trap of the devil, who has taken them captive to do his will.**"* (NIV)

It does not get any clearer than that. This shows a servant of God coming alongside another believer, who has been demonized, and ministering to him with truth and knowledge.

The Christian is provided with armor and complete protection from the fiery darts of the enemy (Ephesians 6). Unfortunately, most believers don't always use their armor. Born-again Christians, including pastors and leaders, are living defeated lives and having many difficulties and problems in which they can find no hope in ever overcoming. Many are discouraged or in despair, and many walk away from God. They quit and give up—which is just what the demons want.

Scripture References Pertaining to Demonized Believers

Believers were shown to be victims of demonic attack in the Scriptures. The physical afflictions and other disasters of Job are shown to be the work of Satan. In the synagogue there was a man with an unclean spirit (Mark 1:23). A woman called "a daughter of Abraham" was bound with a spirit of infirmity for eighteen years (Luke13:11–16). A member of the church in Corinth is shown to have been overcome by a spirit of lust (1 Cor.5:1–5). Sickness is described as an "oppression of the Devil" in Acts 10:38, and Jesus mostly healed by removing spirits of infirmity or unclean spirits.

What about Peter? At one moment he spoke by divine revelation, declaring that "Jesus is the very Christ," and in the next moment, Jesus rebuked Satan using him (Matt. 16:13–23). Simon the magician is mentioned as one who believed and was baptized, but had evidently not been set free from his occult bondages, and was told to repent and pray. He still had a demon attached to him from the occult (Acts 8:20–24). How is it that Satan managed to "fill the hearts" of two believers in the church, Ananias and Sapphira, to lie? (Acts 5:3). Paul himself wrote that he suffered buffeting from a "messenger of Satan", a demon spirit (2 Cor. 12:7). A messenger is an angel, and in this case, a fallen one.

Paul comes against the Corinthian believers for receiving another spirit beside the Spirit they had previously received (2 Cor. 11:4). Since it is not the Holy Spirit, it can only be a demonic one. Paul also inquired, in Galatians 3:1, "who had bewitched the believers to draw them away from the truth?"

Unforgiveness: Giving Away Your Authority

The one biggest cause of demonization in a believer, let alone in an unbeliever, is unforgiveness. Let's look at Mathew 18, verses 32–35. You will discover that God Himself will hand a person over to demons to be tormented. Many overlook this verse.

> **Matthew 18:32–35** *Then summoning him, his lord said to him, You wicked slave, I forgave you all that debt because you pleaded with me. Should you not also have had mercy on your fellow slave, in the same way that I had mercy on you? And his lord, moved with anger, handed him over to the torturers until he should repay all that was owed him. My heavenly Father will also do the same to you, if each of you does not forgive his brother from your heart.*

The demons are pictured as jailers. **They legally have a right to torment a person until the person repents.** God is very serious about holding any unforgiveness toward another person...or in some cases even toward oneself. If you talk to anyone you know that has unforgiveness in them, you know how tormented they are.

Conclusion:

Whether you believe that Christians are demonized from without or within, the cure is still the same: submitting to God and His truths. A person can be free of all demonization if he follows this simple principle. This book will highlight how to do that.

Casting out demon spirits is not something new to the church. It has been misinterpreted, forgotten, and swept aside. Do not dismiss the issue, but research it. Get involved doing what Jesus said to do. We are to cast out demons in His name.

Many believers are destroyed by demons, believing it is just their flesh, and that they cannot change nor have freedom. Remember: God has said, in Hosea 4:6, "My people are destroyed for a lack of knowledge." The lack of knowledge that Christians can—and do—have demons is one way that believers are destroyed today.

$\backsim$ # Chapter 3 $\sim$

◆

Know Your Enemy

"I have been a Christian for 7 years now. My life seems to always be one of defeat and turmoil. I continue to fall victim to the same sins over and over again. This makes me feel inadequate to serve the Lord. No one at my church has an answer. Could you please help me?"

Where Did Satan Come From?

First, we need to understand that God existed in the beginning—not Satan.

> **Genesis 1:1** *In the beginning God created the heavens and the earth.* (NIV)

Second, we should see that God, not Satan, made everything.

> **Exodus 20:11** *For in six days the LORD made the heavens and the earth, the sea, and all that is in them, but he rested on the seventh day. Therefore the LORD blessed the Sabbath day and made it holy.* (NIV)

> **Nehemiah 9:6** *You alone are the LORD. You made the heavens, even the highest heavens, and all their starry host, the earth and all that is on it, the seas and all that is in them. You give life to everything, and the multitudes of heaven worship you.* (NIV)

Third, we should know that God made Satan.

> **Colossians 1:16** *For by him all things were created: things in heaven and on earth, visible and invisible, whether thrones or powers or rulers or authorities; all things were created by him and for him.* (NIV)

Who is Greater: the Creator or the Creation?

I find that many people attribute Satan with too much power or with characteristics that he doesn't have. They talk of him as if he is a god. One must remember that Satan is nothing but an angel created by God, who sinned and rebelled against God. Satan is very limited in what he can do, and even then, he can do only that which God allows.

> **Ezekiel 28:12–19** *Son of man, take up a lament concerning the king of Tyre and say to him: This is what the Sovereign LORD says: "You were the model of perfection, full of wisdom and perfect in beauty. You were in Eden, the garden of God; every precious stone adorned you: ruby, topaz and emerald, chrysolite, onyx and jasper, sapphire, turquoise and beryl. Your settings and mountings were made of gold; on the day you were created they were prepared. You were anointed as a guardian cherub, for so I ordained you. You were on the holy mount of God; you walked among the fiery stones. You were blameless in your ways from the day you were created till wickedness was found in you. Through your widespread trade you were filled with violence, and you sinned. So I drove you in disgrace from the mount of God, and I expelled you, O guardian cherub, from among the fiery stones. Your heart became proud on account of your beauty, and you corrupted your wisdom because of your splendor. So I threw you to the earth; I made a spectacle of you before kings. By your many sins and dishonest trade you have desecrated your sanctuaries. So I made a fire come out from you, and it consumed you, and I reduced you to ashes on the ground in the sight of all who were watching. All the nations who knew you are appalled at you; you have come to a horrible end and will be no more."* (NIV)

Ezekiel speaks in this passage about the king of Tyrus; however, the passage has a double meaning. It describes the literal king of Tyrus, but it also describes Satan ("Lucifer" was Satan's name before he sinned), as Dr. Charles C. Ryrie explains in his book, *Basic Theology:* [4]

> It would, of course, not be unusual for a prophetic passage to refer both to a local personage and also to someone else who fully fulfills it. This is true of many passages that relate both to King David and Jesus Christ. It is also true of

the reference to the prince of the kingdom of Persia in Daniel 10:13, a reference that must include a superhuman being related to the kingdom of Persia. So for Ezekiel 28 to refer both to the then-reigning king of Tyre as well as to Satan would not be a unique interpretive conclusion. Indeed, it seems the right conclusion: The historic king of Tyre was simply a tool of Satan, possibly indwelt by him. And in describing this king, Ezekiel also gives us glimpses of the superhuman creature, Satan, who was using, if not indwelling, him.

God the Creator made (literally, "set") Lucifer to be full of wisdom and perfect in beauty. He was complete. God also set him in the Garden of Eden. This points back to Satan's origin (see Genesis 3:1).

God covered him with every precious stone. Actually, this list is the same as the list of stones on the apparel of the high priest, with the exception of three stones. The gold is specifically representative of kingly apparel. The mercy seat in the temple was made of pure gold. The idea of "workmanship" indicates that God had made Lucifer for a specific service. The idea of him being "prepared" indicates that God designed him for a specific purpose.

Lucifer was the anointed cherub that covered God's throne. The word "anointed" means "to be set apart for service unto God." God said that Lucifer was upon the Holy Mountain of God. This was the place set apart, or exalted, for God. Satan (Lucifer) was in the presence of God walking up and down in the middle of the stones of fire.

Satan was created perfect in his ways, his thoughts, and his actions from the time God created him. Then iniquity was found in him. The word "iniquity" means "perverseness."

God bluntly said that Satan had sinned. God said he expelled Satan from the Mountain of God. God is still, and always will be, in control. Because of Satan's pride, God said that He would bring judgment upon Satan. Because of Satan's iniquity (perverseness), and his spreading of that iniquity, God will judge him with fire.

Isaiah 14:12–14 *How you have fallen from heaven, O morning star, son of the dawn! You have been cast down to* *the earth, you who once laid low the nations! You said in your heart, "I will ascend to heaven; I will raise my throne above the stars of God; I will sit enthroned on the mount of assembly, on the utmost heights of the sacred mountain. I will ascend above the tops of the clouds; I will make myself like the Most High."* (NIV)

Lucifer is the original name given to the devil. The term "Lucifer" means the "Shining One." This is very interesting because we can see that God created Lucifer (Satan) to reflect God's glory. Ironically, now he only appears as an angel of light; but in fact, he is the angel of darkness.

There are five "*I wills*" listed in the previous passage from Isaiah. These indicate his pride, his boasting, and his foolishness. Lucifer *assumed* authority—in contrast to *receiving* God's *delegated* authority:

1. "I will ascend to heaven"
    –He assumes to take the abode of God.

2. "I will raise my throne above the stars of God"
    –This may indicate taking authority over all of God's angels (Job 38:7).

3. "I will sit enthroned on the mount of assembly"
    –This refers to the temple (Daniel 11:37, 2 Thessalonians 2:4).

4. "I will ascend above the heights of the clouds"
    –The cloud is a covering of God (Exodus 13:21).

5. "I will make myself like the most high"
    –He assumed to take the place of God.

God has brought judgment upon Satan. When Satan's judgment is revealed, people will marvel: not at his power, but at his deceptiveness in *appearing* to have power.

What are His Names?

Abaddon	Revelation 9:11
Accuser of the brethren	Revelation 12:10
Adversary (one who stands against)	1 Peter 5:8
Angel of the bottomless pit	Revelation 9:11
Antichrist (the one against Christ)	1 John 4:3
Apollyon (Greek; Destroyer)	Revelation 9:11
Beelzebul (god of the flies, dung god)	Matthew 12:24, Mark 3:22, Luke 11:15
Belial	2 Corinthians 6:15
Destroyer	1 Corinthians 10:10, Jeremiah 51:1
Devil (false accuser, devil, slanderer)	Matthew 4:1, Luke 4:2, 6; Revelation 20:2
Enemy	Matthew 13:39
Evil spirit	1 Samuel 16:14
Father of all lies (a liar)	John 8:44
god of this world	2 Corinthians 4:4
Great red dragon	Revelation 12:3
Lucifer (Roman rendering of "morning star")	Isaiah 14:12
Man of sin	2 Thessalonians 2:3
Murderer	John 8:44
Old serpent	Revelation 12:9, Revelation 20:2
Power of darkness	Colossians 1:13
Prince of this world	John 12:31, John 14:30, John 16:11
Prince of the power of the air	Ephesians 2:2
Tempter	Matthew 4:3; 1 Thessalonians 3:5
Thief	John 10:10
Wicked one	Matthew 13:19, 38
Ruler of darkness (understood as)	Ephesians 6:12

Satan (Hebrew means "adversary"; Greek means "accuser")	1 Chronicles 21:1, Job 1:6, John 13:27, Acts 5:3, Acts 26:18, Romans 16:20
Serpent	Genesis 3:4, 14; 1 Corinthians 11:3
Son of perdition (destruction, ruin, waste, loss)	John 17:12
The unholy trinity is the devil, the beast, and the false prophet	Revelation 20:10

What is Satan's Strategy?

He lies in wait to overcome the believer. He schemes, and he plots an attack.

> **Ephesians 6:11** *Put on the full armor of God so that you can take your stand against the <u>devil's schemes</u>.* (NIV)

Satan tries to get control of the believer's mind and thoughts.

> **2 Corinthians 2:11** *in order that Satan might not outwit us. For we are not unaware of his schemes.* (NIV)

He comes to steal, kill, and destroy.

> **John 10:10** *The thief comes only to steal and kill and destroy; I have come that they may have life, and have it to the full.* (NIV)

This is his ultimate desire and purpose. What does he seek to steal, kill, and destroy in your life?

The Three Basic Tactics Satan Uses

1) He blinds the minds of unbelievers.

> **2 Corinthians 4:3–4** *And even if our gospel is veiled, it is veiled to those who are perishing. The god of this age has blinded the minds of unbelievers, so that they cannot see the light of the gospel of the glory of Christ, who is the image of God.* (NIV)

On various occasions, I have seen people who say that they could not make a decision for Christ because they were too confused. After praying to God and commanding the spirit of confusion to be bound, many of these individuals readily made decisions to commit their lives to Christ, since they were then able to understand the Gospel message.

2) He assaults the believer's mind.

> **Ephesians 6:12** *For our struggle is not against flesh and blood, but against the rulers, against the authorities, against the powers of this dark world and against the spiritual forces of evil in the heavenly realms.* (NIV)

> **Zechariah 3:1** *Then he showed me Joshua the high priest standing before the angel of the LORD, and Satan standing at his right side to accuse him.* (NIV)

> **Galatians 3:1–2** *You foolish Galatians! Who has bewitched you? Before your very eyes Jesus Christ was clearly portrayed as crucified. I would like to learn just one thing from you: Did you receive the Spirit by observing the law, or by believing what you heard?* (NIV)

Many believers are led into captivity in this area. They begin to see themselves as having to work to attain a standard of self-righteousness. They disregard the grace gift that Jesus gives us, such as his imputed righteousness to all believers.

3) He tempts men to sin.

Genesis 3:1–6   *Now the serpent was more crafty than any of the wild animals the LORD God had made. He said to the woman, "Did God really say, 'You must not eat from any tree in the garden'?"*
The woman said to the serpent, "We may eat fruit from the trees in the garden, but God did say, 'You must not eat fruit from the tree that is in the middle of the garden, and you must not touch it, or you will die.'"
"You will not surely die," the serpent said to the woman. "For God knows that when you eat of it your eyes will be opened, and you will be like God, knowing good and evil."
When the woman saw that the fruit of the tree was good for food and pleasing to the eye, and also desirable for gaining wisdom, she took some and ate it. She also gave some to her husband, who was with her, and he ate it. (NIV)

1 Chronicles 21:1   *Satan rose up against Israel and incited David to take a census of Israel.* (NIV)

Matthew 4:1   *Then Jesus was led by the Spirit into the desert to be tempted by the devil* (NIV)

Satan tries to take the authority away from a believer by getting him to offer himself up to sin.

What are Satan's Methods of Attack?

GENERAL METHODS:

1. Enticement (curious arts and the occult)

Acts 19:19   *A number who had practiced sorcery brought their scrolls together and burned them publicly. When they calculated the value of the scrolls, the total came to fifty thousand drachmas.* (NIV)

See also; Leviticus 19:31, Deuteronomy 18:10-11

2. Oppression (outside attack; to press against, down, under)

> **Acts 10:38** *how God anointed Jesus of Nazareth with the Holy Spirit and power, and how he went around doing good and healing all who were under the power of the devil, because God was with him.* (NIV)

See also Isaiah 52:4

3. Demonization

> **2 Timothy 2:26** *and that they will come to their senses and escape from the trap of the devil, who has taken them captive to do his will.* (NIV)

SPECIFIC METHODS:

1. He uses surprise, as a thief would. John 10:10

2. He attacks at the point of our weakness. 1 John 2:16

3. He attacks at the point of our strengths. 1 Chronicles 21:1

4. He uses aggression. 1 Peter 5:8 (Isaiah 5:29), Matthew 11:12

5. He steals the good seed of the Word. Matthew 13:19

6. He sows tares (the children of evil). Matthew 13:38–39

7. He inflicts disease. Job 2:7, Luke 13:16

8. He initiates death and destruction. Job 1:12–19

9. He brings accusations against believers. Revelation 12:10

10. He induces mental and emotional disorders. Mark 5:1–6

What are Satan's Weapons?

1. **Appearing as an angel of light** - 2 Corinthians 11:14
2. **Darkness** - Ephesians 6:12, Luke 22:53
3. **Deception** - 2 Thessalonians 2:10, Psalm 10:7, Romans 3:13
4. **Intimidation** - 1 Samuel 17:4–11 (Goliath), Nehemiah 4:1–3
5. **Ignorance** - Hosea 4:6, Romans 10:3
6. **Confusion** - Acts 19:23–29 ("I don't understand")
7. **Doubt** (questioning) – Gen. 3:1, Acts 12:14–15 ("Do you think…")

More of the Enemy's Weapons:	*In Contrast With the Believer's:*
Lies (deception and confusion) -Genesis 3:4, 1 Kings 13:18	**Truth**
Unrighteousness (wrong thoughts) -2 Thessalonians 2:10	**Righteousness**
Condemnation (accusation) -Job 4:17–18, Nehemiah 6:6	**Gospel of peace**
Fear (worry, anxiety) -Job 4:14–15	**Faith**
Destruction -John 10:10, 1 Corinthians 5:5	**Salvation**
Another word (traditions, opinions, doctrines) -Galatians 1:6–8	**Word of God**
Distractions (entertainment, addictions, laziness) -Judges 14:1–3	**Prayer**
Division (separation, disunity) -Jude 1:19	**Reconciliation**

How Does Satan Set Up Strongholds?

The soul of man (the mind, will, and emotions) is like a house (Matthew 12: 43–45). The enemy is like a wild animal: crouched and ready to spring into any opening he can find (Genesis 4:7). If a believer is not careful to keep sin "doors" closed to Satan, he will come in, and attempt to take dominion in that area. Here are some of the main doorways:

- **Anger**

    Ephesians 4:26–27 *Be angry, and yet do not sin; do not let the sun go down on your anger, and do not give the devil an opportunity.*

    Ephesians 4:31–32 *Get rid of all bitterness, rage and anger, brawling and slander, along with every form of malice. Be kind and compassionate to one another, forgiving each other, just as in Christ God forgave you.* (NIV)

Anger is a God-given emotion. However, anger must be dealt with quickly. Believers who remain angry give an opportunity for the enemy to exploit it. The enemy will then begin to take control of one or more areas of the believer's life.

- **Unforgiveness**

    Matthew 18:34–35 *In anger his master turned him over to the jailers to be tortured, until he should pay back all he owed. "This is how my heavenly Father will treat each of you unless you forgive your brother from your heart."* (NIV)

This passage shows:

- Unforgiveness opens the door to evil spirits.
- Evil spirits are described here as the "torturers or tormentors".
- God is described as "The King," who is willing to forgive.
- However, when the believer does not fully accept (and apply!)

the grace of forgiveness, he then holds unforgiveness toward others.

• When a person holds unforgiveness toward any fellow man, God turns them over to the tormentors (evil spirits) to harass, control, and discipline them.

My experience has taught me that unforgiveness may lead to bitterness, rage, revenge, guilt, depression, and even to suicide. The longer the person is unwilling to forgive, the more severe these get.

• **Bitterness**

> **Hebrews 12:15** *See to it that no one misses the grace of God and that no bitter root grows up to cause trouble and defile many.* (NIV)

Bitterness not only defiles the one holding it, but causes others to become defiled as well. It becomes trouble for all involved.

• **Occult involvement**

> **Leviticus 19:31** *Do not turn to mediums or spiritists; do not seek them out to be defiled by them. I am the LORD your God.*

Any type of occult involvement opens the doors. Some examples are: witchcraft, psychics, use of Ouija boards, horoscopes, palm reading, Harry Potter, and Poke'mon.

Using the Ouija board would result in more demonic activity than reading Harry Potter since it is a direct tool. Occult demons are some of the strongest demons besides sexual demons. Once the door is open to them, they then seek to draw the person deeper into occult activities. This explains why one who starts out with horoscopes is then led deeper by seeking psychics or tarot card readings. The draw of power and knowledge is pleasing to the flesh.

What is Satan's Power?

1. Satan's power is limited.
   a) He is limited in his power of destruction (Job 1:9–12).
   b) He is limited in his ability to bring temptations (1 Corinthians 10:13).

2. Satan's power is real.
   a) He beguiled Eve (2 Corinthians 11:3).
   b) He uses magical powers (Exodus 7:11–12).
   c) He empowered a witch to bring forth a spirit (1 Samuel 28:12–20).
   d) He wars against the angels of God (Daniel 10:13).
   e) He is called a god of forces (Daniel 11:13).

3. He is given power to war with the tribulation saints (Revelation 13:7).

4. He has power to cause people to worship the beast (Revelation 13:12–15)

What is Satan's Destination?

   1) He is restrained until the Holy Spirit is removed from earth (2 Thessalonians 2:7–11)
   2) He is to enter a man and deceive the world (2 Thessalonians 2:3–6).
   3) He comes to the earth with fury, as he knows his time is short (Revelation 12:9–12).
   4) He is bound for a thousand years then loosed for a season (Revelation 20:1–9).
   5) He is cast into the lake of fire (Matthew 25:41, Revelation 20:10).

Now that you understand the enemy, you can begin to see why faith in God and his truth makes practical sense. Satan has nothing of any value in a believer's life.

Chapter 4

◆

Demons' Plans And Strategies

"I am just a big mass of confusion. I want to serve the Lord and do what He wants me to do. I want to be the person I am supposed to be. But I am not. I live in constant fear."

I n the previous chapter, we learned about our enemy, Satan. We discovered what his strategies and tactics are, what he uses for weapons, and how he uses opportunity in the lives of believers. We learned how much power he has (or only appears to have), and we learned what his final destiny is.

But it is important to understand that Satan is not our only enemy. In any war, the commander-in-chief operates as the brains behind the operation; the actual plans are mostly carried out by the soldiers beneath him. Just as in human armies and war, Satan has his own "soldiers": demons.

We need to learn more about demons so that we can stand against them effectively.

Whether you are a believer or an unbeliever, demons have strategies for keeping you out of God's will. The lost people of the world, as well as the majority of Christians today, are ignorant of the reality of evil spirits (demons). Most believers would prefer that they were not talked about or even mentioned. They want to ignore this part of God's Word, because they are afraid of things that they were misled into thinking. The result of living in such ignorance of the spiritual realm is that multitudes of believers and unbelievers live in needless torment and defeat.

Demons are spirits. They are invisible to the human eye, although they can manifest at times. I myself have witnessed actual manifestations on numerous occasions. They have an evil, wicked intelligence that seeks out bodies in which they can express themselves through. They are emissaries sent from Satan's kingdom, possessing personalities and characteristics that make up an intelligent spirit being. They are able to walk, hear, speak, see, obey or disobey, deceive, lie, seek out, think, and make decisions. They can dwell in humans, as seen in the verse below:

> **Matthew 12:43–45** *Now when the unclean spirit goes out of a man, it passes through waterless places seeking rest, and does not find it. Then it says, "I will return to my house from which I came;" and when it comes, it finds it unoccupied, swept, and put in order. Then it goes and takes along with it seven other spirits more wicked than itself, and they go in and live there; and the last state of that man becomes worse than the first. That is the way it*

will also be with this evil generation.

They demonize, or dwell, in a body to accomplish their evil purposes. Every demon has a certain function and mission, which one can learn to recognize by the fruit it bears or manifests in the victim.

What Are Evil Spirits (Demons)?

1. They were created by God (originally created as good, in that God created everything.) - Colossians 1:16
2. They were with God as angels - Revelation 12:4
3. Fallen angels became evil spirits.
    a) Luke 10:18 (see also Matthew 25:41)
    b) Revelation 12:3–4 (see also Daniel 8:10)
    c) Revelation 12:7–9
4. The worst of the worst.
    a) They left their first estate (as angels). - Jude 6
    b) Satan persuaded some demons to cohabit with woman. - Genesis 6:4

Some Evil Spirits Listed in Scripture

Familiar spirit (1 Samuel 28:7)	A spirit (Job 4:15)
Spirit of deep sleep (Isaiah 29:10)	Spirit of whoredoms (Hosea 4:12)
Unclean spirit (Luke 8:29)	Spirit of infirmity (Luke 13:11)
Spirit of divination (Acts 16:16)	Spirit of bondage (Romans 8:15)
Enticing spirit (2 Chronicles 18:20)	Spirit of devils (Revelation 16:14)
Spirits of false prophets (1 John 4:1)	Seducing spirits (1 Timothy 4:1)
Evil spirits (Acts 19:13)	Angel of light (2 Corinthians 11:14)
The tormentors (Matthew 18:34)	Devil (Ephesians 4:27, Luke 9:42)
Devils (Luke 11:20)	A god of forces (Daniel 11:38)
Prince of Persia (Daniel 10:13)	Spirit of fear (2 Timothy 1:7)
Spirit of antichrist (1 John 4:3)	Spirit of error (1 John 4:6)
Foul spirit (Revelation 18:2)	Prince of the power of the air (Ephesians 2:2)
Another spirit (2 Corinthians 11:4)	Spirit of the world (1 Corinthians 2:12)
Unclean devil (Luke 4:33)	Dumb spirit (Mark 9:17)
Spirit of heaviness (Isaiah 61:3)	Perverse spirit (Isaiah 19:14)
A haughty spirit (Proverbs 16:18)	
Spirit of jealousy (Numbers 5:14)	

Some Additional Spirits that I Have Personally Encountered
(These are but a few)

Death	Furcus	Rejection	Unforgiveness
Suicide	Deception	Amon	Shiva
Abdiel	Hadorym	Mockery	Azeal
Terminator	Baalberith	Abaddon	Necrophilia
Destroyer	Self Hate	Hate	Dahlia
Striker	Orobus	Lust	Homosexuality
Incubus	Sydonay	Fear	Bestiality
Malphas	Rage	Anger	

Another good resource for demonic names during encounters can be found in Dr. Ed Murphy's book, *The Handbook For Spiritual Warfare*, Thomas Nelson Publishers, 1992.

A Brief Look at What Demons Do To the Believer

1) Demons use deception.

They use lies and twisted truths of God's word. If a believer lacks knowledge of Biblical truth and doctrines, he can easily be deceived into doctrinal errors; such as thinking one can lose their salvation. This false teaching keeps one in a circle of torment, doubt, and legalism. This believer is always frustrated in trying to "do good" to obtain favorable standing with God.

Others are deceived to focus on the gifts of the Holy Spirit, rather than on the One who gives the gifts. This leads to glorifying the Holy Spirit, as well as self. The Bible clearly shows that the Holy Spirit never glorifies Himself, yet always brings glory to Jesus, and Jesus always brings glory to the Father. The Holy Spirit is never to be glorified and man is to be always humble, never lifted up in pride. Much of this goes back to the Garden of Eden, "Did God really say that?"

2) Demons use ignorance.

If a believer is ignorant of God's word, the believer is easily led away to destruction and defeat. If one is ignorant of the truth, he will only be able to respond to lies. Many are ignorant of the truths contained in the pages of this book. A believer must begin to know who God is, who the enemy is, and who the believer is in Christ. To overcome ignorance, studying and praying over God's word is a must.

3) Demons use fear.

A believer lives in fear when he does not know or accept the written promises of God's word. A believer is to walk by faith and not by sight. Most believers seem to put their trust in what the enemy says, rather than in what God has said.

4) Demons use false teachings.

Besides doctrinal errors, there are two main false teachings in the church today in regards to demonic activity. First, that a believer should not be concerned with thoughts that a demon could be their problem. Second, that a believer in Christ cannot be demonized. These false teachings allow the Devil and his demon army a "freedom" to bring fear, mental torment, jealousy, hatred, lust, pride, self-pity, addictions, oppression, depression, unforgiveness, and many other forms of bondage…all undetected by the Body of Christ. These teachings are a part of Satan's strategy to undermine God's people and take them captive.

5) Demons use sin areas.

Satan and demons have no power over a believer unless that believer gives it to them. A believer with knowledge realizes that he can stand in victory over them with the power and authority of Christ. If a believer continues to practice willful sin, Satan will send one or more of his demonic agents that is compatible with that particular sin. The demon will dwell with the believer, tempting him to engage in that sin more. Then each time the believer gives into that sin, the demon spirit takes over in assisting the believer to carry it out. Demon personalities knit very tightly with the victims, and it requires some spiritual discernment to expose them. Demons attach themselves to "sin areas" of a believer's life, and work continually to increase control or domination of those areas. This is demonization.

A person is demonized when they become hopeless and defeated in an area of their life, such as with unforgiveness or addictions.

6) Demons attack the mind.

Demons have many attack strategies they can use to undermine the faith of a believer. However, the mind of a person is the main focus of attack. They will plant thoughts in the unguarded mind of a believer and intensify the evil that is already in one's human nature.

Satan and his demons assault the believer's mind with doubts and fears. They put forth challenges to the believer's faith and undermine his confidence in God's goodness and promises. A believer will then have perceived inconsistencies, or vain imaginations, in God's treatment of His people or others. A believer must learn to stop the demonic assault by rejecting their false accusations against God in his mind.

A believer must submit or take captive every thought and make it obedient to Jesus Christ.

> **2 Corinthians 10:5** *"We are destroying speculations and every lofty thing raised up against the knowledge of God, and we are taking every thought captive to the obedience of Christ,"*

Once a believer is deceived in their mind by demons into doubting God's goodness and promises, then the believer will automatically doubt God's Word as well. This renders the believer powerless. They have believed the lies of the enemy instead of God—who is the source of all truth.

Demons are sly and subtle. They use doorways of sin and disobedience to their advantage and even use generational sins as well. We will look at generational sin later in Chapter 11.

Doorways are opened to demons when a believer steps out of submitting his mind and/or body to the Lordship of Jesus Christ. When a believer sins in this way and does not choose to turn to God in repentance, he then becomes open for demonic attack and dominion. This particular sin could have initially been conceived either by a demonic spirit or the believer's own fleshly natural desires. The demons want to lead believers into captivity to do their will (2 Timothy 2:25–26). A believer will become so preoccupied with his sin that it will cause him to feel that he is not worthy to serve God.

Demons are crafty liars, deceivers, and twisters of God's truths. They will seek to destroy a believer's abundant life and walk with God, to make him ineffective for the kingdom of God.

What Do Demons Do To Those Who Don't Believe?

1) They use deception.

Demons love to keep the unbeliever trapped in their unbelief. They do not care if a person follows all the adverse religions and false beliefs of the world. If a person is deceived into thinking they are okay, and that they might make it to heaven, then the demons will perpetuate this. In reality, the demons know that following any belief except faith in Jesus Christ alone will make one destined for an eternity in Hell. Deception and blindness to the truth of Jesus Christ is the game plan for unbelievers.

There is only one way to God, not many—even if the other ways appear to be godly. That's the deception. Not because I said so, but because God has said it. Jesus, who is God, said:

> **Matthew 7:13–14** *"Enter through the narrow gate; for the gate is wide and the way is broad that leads to destruction, and there are many who enter through it. For the gate is small and the way is narrow that leads to life, and there are few who find it."*

There are not many paths to God, only one. It's His way; not yours, not mine, not anyone else's way. If you are an unbeliever reading this book, my intent is to give you truth.

You are caught in false doctrines and/or religions if you follow teachings such as these listed here:

- Jehovah's Witness
- The Catholic Church
- Scientology
- Seventh Day Adventists
- Mormonism
- The Masonic Lodge
- Spiritualism
- Hinduism
- Islam (Muslims)
- All Occult Activities (Wicca, Witchcraft, Satanism, etc.)
- Evolutionism
- U.F.O. teachings
- Any and all teachings or belief systems other than the Lord Jesus Christ alone.

If you are involved with any of these, you have been taken captive by Satan's kingdom.

Now I do love all, and I have warned you because I care. I know it may be hard to accept, and just as hard to know that you must reject years of traditions that have been handed down. I speak the truth of God and not of my own accord, to warn you of your needless destruction. Know the truth and the truth will set you free.

Whatever you have been seeking is only found in a *relationship* with the one who is Truth: Jesus Christ the Lord. Seek Him and Him alone. Repent, turn to God, and leave the futile thinking and demonic lies behind you. Be transferred from Satan's kingdom to God's kingdom!

2) They inflict pain and suffering.

Demons promote pain and suffering in the world. This helps perpetuate the lie that God does not exist. Abuse and pain cause division and strife. Families hurt each other and sins can be passed down through generations as a curse upon the children (see Chapter 11). The demons enslave people to selfishness, unworthiness, unforgiveness, molestation, and emotional and sexual abuse. They promote the idea of "do whatever you want no matter who you hurt." Demons use people to hurt other people. They seek to destroy families and relationships, and to pervert God's creation.

Now that you understand the deceptive tactics demons use against you, you can begin to recognize when—and how—they attack you. Whatever area in your life they attack around, apply God's truth to it. Stand in the truth, and stay free.

Chapter 5

◆

Knowing God...Who Is He?

"I never really understood how much God loved me— or why— before my deliverance. I was always rejected by others and felt unloved. I have learned to trust God based on His written promises, rather than on my feelings."

W e serve a mighty and awesome God. God is *the* absolute power, authority, and ruler. I felt it was necessary to demonstrate this from the Scriptures. The truths in this chapter are important to understand, for we are in Him, and He is in us when we know Jesus Christ as Savior. This is part of our identity in Christ, and the source of what is available, by faith, to us that know Him.

As a believer, God's awesome power and authority is the very essence that courses throughout our being. The believer can stand in God's power in spiritual warfare against Satan and his demons. In later chapters, our authority and weapons will be discussed in more detail. By comprehending the power and authority behind our weapons, the believer can stand in faith and confidence in all areas of life, but especially in spiritual warfare.

God Was in the Beginning

Genesis 1:1 *"In the beginning God created the heavens and the earth."*

"In the beginning God..." All other philosophies or religions of man begin with man in search of a God (if there is one), or trying to get to God. But He is the creator of all things.

John 1:1–3 *"In the beginning was the Word, and the Word was with God, and the Word was God. The same was in the beginning with God. All things were made by him; and without him was not any thing made that was made."*

This is a reference to Jesus Christ. Everything that was made was made by Him. This means all ownership and authority is His alone.

God is Total

"I AM." God is all and all, and no names can compare to Him. He just is.

Revelation 1:8, 11 *"I am the Alpha and the Omega," says the Lord God, "who is and who was and who is to come, the Almighty."*

Colossians 1:17 *"He is before all things, and in Him all things hold together."*

He is The One and Only God

Deuteronomy 4:35 *"To you it was shown that you might know that the Lord, He is God; there is no other besides Him."*

Deuteronomy 6:4 *"Hear, O Israel! The Lord is our God, the Lord is one!"*

Psalm 86:10 *"For You are great and do wondrous deeds; you alone are God."*

2 Samuel 7:22 *"For this reason You are great, Oh Lord God; for there is none like You, and there is no God besides You, according to all that we have heard with our ears."*

No Other God Exists Before or After Him

God is called Jehovah. In the Hebrew this translates as Yahweh, or "the One who is"

Isaiah 43:10 *"You are my witnesses," declares the LORD, "and my servant whom I have chosen, so that you may know and believe me and understand that I am he. Before me no god was formed, nor will there be one after me."* (NIV)

Isaiah 46:9–10 *Remember the former things, those of long ago; I am God, and there is no other; I am God, and* *there is none like me. I make known the end from the beginning, from ancient times, what is still to come. I say: My purpose will stand, and I will do all that I please.* (NIV)

God is One God

Psalm 83:18 *Let them know that you, whose name is the LORD, that you alone are the Most High over all the earth.* (NIV)

Mark 12:29 *Jesus answered, "The foremost is, 'HEAR, O ISRAEL! THE LORD OUR GOD IS ONE LORD;..."*

1 Corinthians 8:4–6 *So then, about eating food sacrificed to idols: We know that an idol is nothing at all in the world and that there is no God but one. For even if there are so-called gods, whether in heaven or on earth (as indeed there are many "gods" and many "lords"), yet for us there is but one God, the Father, from whom all things came and for whom we live; and there is but one Lord, Jesus Christ, through whom all things came and through whom we live.* (NIV)

We must understand that the Bible teaches God is three-in-one. This is called the doctrine of the trinity.

Trinity: Webster's Dictionary gives the following definition of trinity: "The union of three divine persons (or hypostases), the Father, Son, and Holy Spirit, in one divinity, so that all the three are one God as to substance, but three Persons (or hypostases as to individuality)." Synonyms sometimes used are triunity, trine, triality. The term "trinity" is formed from "tri," three, and "nity," unity. Triunity is a better term than "trinity" because it better expresses the idea of three in one. God is three in one. "Hypostases" is the plural of "*hypostasis,*" which means "the substance, the underlying reality, or essence."

The doctrine of the trinity states that there is one God who is one in essence or substance, but three in personality. This does not mean three independent Gods existing as one, but three Persons who are co-equal, co eternal, inseparable, interdependent, and eternally united in one absolute Divine Essence and Being.

God is Eternal

> **Deuteronomy 33:27** *The eternal God is your refuge, and underneath are the everlasting arms. He will drive out your enemy before you, saying, Destroy him!* (NIV)

> **Hebrews 13:8** *Jesus Christ is the same yesterday and today and forever.* (NIV)

Note: God never changes!

The Kingdom of God is Sovereign and Eternal

> **Psalm 45:6** *Your throne, O God, will last for ever and ever; a scepter of justice will be the scepter of your kingdom.* (NIV)

> **Psalm 47:2** *How awesome is the LORD Most High, the great King over all the earth.* (NIV)

> **Daniel 4:17** *The decision is announced by messengers, the holy ones declare the verdict, so that the living may know that the Most High is sovereign over the kingdoms of men and gives them to anyone he wishes and sets over them the lowliest of men.* (NIV)

Governments and world leaders rise and fall, but God remains The Sovereign forever.

Identifying Names for God

Names are important. This is especially true in the Bible, where names are used to identify authority, character, purpose, or relationship.

Meaning of names:

a. One in authority gives a name. Genesis 2:19, 2 Kings 23:34
b. The name often indicates a relationship between the person and the one who gives the name. Genesis 35:18, 2 Samuel 12:24
c. The name usually denotes the character of the person. 1 Samuel 25:25
d. The name usually gives the purpose of person. (e.g. "Moses" = "Draw Out")
e. To dishonor the name is to dishonor the person. (e.g., forgetting a name is akin to forgetting the person) Jeremiah 23:27, Matthew 28:19, 1 Corinthians 1:13, 15
f. To rightfully use the name of another is to use their authority. 2 Corinthians 5:20

Names of God in Scripture:

El—(Hebrew for God) - mighty one. Genesis 14:18. A common term for God.

Elohiym—object of worship (plural form). Genesis 1:1, from "Alah" - meaning to swear. This form is listed 2,570 times (Genesis 1:26, Psalm 110:4, Titus 1:2). Believers understand that there is one God made known in three persons: the Father, the Son, and the Holy Spirit.

I AM—(English rendering for "self existing one" = Yahweh) - Exodus 3:14

Jehovah (Hebrew =Yahweh) – "the One who is" - LORD - Please understand that the Israelites were afraid to speak the name of God for fear of using His name in vain. Therefore, there was a substitution with "LORD".

Jehovah-jireh - God who provides. Genesis 22:14 (Philippians 4:19)

Jehovah-rapha - God heals. Exodus 15:26 (Deuteronomy 7:15)

Jehovah-nissi - God is my banner. Exodus 17:15 (2 Chronicles 20:17)

Jehovah-m'kaddesh - God who sanctifies. ("to sanctify" means "to set apart," usually for service) Leviticus 20:7

Jehovah-shalom - God of peace. Judges 6:24 (Isaiah 26:3)

Jehovah-tsidkenu - God our righteousness. Jeremiah 23:5–6 (Galatians 3:6)

Jehovah-rohi - God my shepherd. Psalm 23:1

Jehovah-shammah - God who is there. Ezekiel 48:35 (Psalm 139:7–8)

Some Other Names Given to God in the Bible

Name	Found in:
Almighty (Hebrew "El Shaddai")	Genesis 17:1
Eternal God.	Deuteronomy 33:27
Father of Lights	James 1:17
Holy One of Israel	Psalm 71:22
Fortress	2 Samuel 22:2
Living God	Joshua 3:10
Heavenly Father.	Matthew 6:26
Lord of Lords.	Deuteronomy 10:27
Lord of Hosts.	1 Samuel 1:11
Lord of Sabbath	James 5:4
Judge	Genesis 18:25
King of Glory	Psalm 24:9–10
Our Father	1 Chronicles 29:10, Matthew 6:9
Most High	Deuteronomy 32:8

What are God's Plans?

The revelation of God's plans for His creation is only partial; this is by divine design for the purpose of God. Some things are "revealed" and some things still remain "secret." The "secret things belong to God," we are told in Scripture.

> **Deuteronomy 29:29** *The secret things belong to the LORD our God, but the things revealed belong to us and to our sons forever, that we may observe all the words of this law.*

The secrets are not for us to know at this time. Only the things that have been revealed are for us. They are for us to know, to understand, to meditate upon, and to explore.

Specifically, they are revealed to us so that we might know and obey God's commands. The written Word of God is the knowledge He has chosen to reveal and give to us. Ultimately everything is for God's glory. Your life is for glorifying God. The deliverance of a person from demons brings glory to God.

Below are just a few specifics about God's plans:

1) God came to destroy Satan's kingdom.

> **1 John 3:8** *He who does what is sinful is of the devil, because the devil has been sinning from the beginning. The reason the Son of God appeared was to destroy the devil's work.* (NIV)

2) God opens the minds of unbelievers.

> **Luke 1:77–79** *...to give his people the knowledge of salvation through the forgiveness of their sins, because of the tender mercy of our God, by which the rising sun will come to us from heaven to shine on those living in darkness and in the shadow of death, to guide our feet into the path of peace.* (NIV)

> **Acts 26:18** *...to open their eyes and turn them from darkness to light, and from the power of Satan to God, so that they may receive forgiveness of sins and a place among those who are*

sanctified by faith in me. (NIV)

The minds of unbelievers have been darkened by the devil, but God's work is to open them to the gospel of Christ. The unbeliever cannot even know the things of God unless God reveals it to him.

3) God seeks and saves the lost.

Matthew 1:21 *She will give birth to a son, and you are to give him the name Jesus, because he will save his people from their sins.* (NIV)

Luke 19:10 *For the Son of Man came to seek and to save what was lost.* (NIV)

This is the purpose of Jesus, even found in the meaning of his name.

4) God enables believers to live (without being a slave to sin) by His grace.

1 Corinthians 10:13 *No temptation has seized you except what is common to man. And God is faithful; he will not let you be tempted beyond what you can bear. But when you are tempted, he will also provide a way out so that you can stand up under it.* (NIV)

Galatians 5:16 *So I say, live by the Spirit, and you will not gratify the desires of the sinful nature.* (NIV)

A believer who walks in the Spirit will not sin. Walking in the Spirit and walking in the flesh are mutually exclusive. One cannot do both at the same time.

5) God gives believers an inheritance in Himself.

Acts 20:32 *"Now I commit you to God and to the word of his grace, which can build you up and give you an inheritance* *among all those who are sanctified."* (NIV)

Romans 8:17 *and if children, heirs also, heirs of God and fellow heirs with Christ, if indeed we suffer with Him so that we may also be glorified with Him.*

Colossians 1:12 *giving thanks to the Father, who has qualified you to share in the inheritance of the saints in the kingdom of light.* (NIV)

2 Corinthians 1:20 *For no matter how many promises God has made, they are "Yes" in Christ. And so through him the "Amen" is spoken by us to the glory of God.* (NIV)

We only breezed the surface of the nature and character of God. The greater your knowledge of God, the greater your faith will be. The more we understand about God, the less we will doubt, the less we will fear, the less we will suffer anxiety, and the less we will feel alone. He is our all-sufficiency and He constantly desires to impart to us any good and perfect gift.

How wonderful it is to know that this all-powerful, all-sufficient God created us to have intimacy with Him. Our completeness can only be fully found when we enter into relationship with Almighty God through the Lord Jesus Christ.

Chapter 6

◆

Believer's Authority

"After spending some carpet time yesterday with God, He just really, really, really, stressed the authority and power I have in and through Him. That was something the enemy tried to deceive me with. He tried to hold me captive and suppressed. Although I have walked in authority before, the devil was trying his best, which is his worst. He will not hold me down, not now, or ever again. I will now laugh in the face of adversity. Instead of being fearful, I will stand firm on who I am in Christ."

W e will now see, from God's Word, how and why a Believer has authority over Satan and his demons through Jesus Christ **(not of your own authority)**. We are going to be referring to the Scripture verses Luke10:17–20; but in particular, verse 19:

> *"The seventy-two returned with joy and said, 'Lord, even the demons submit to us **in your name.**' He replied, 'I saw Satan fall like lightning from heaven. **I have given you authority to trample on snakes and scorpions [demons] and to overcome all the power of the enemy;** nothing will harm you. However, do not rejoice that the spirits submit to you, but rejoice that your names are written in heaven.'"*
> (NIV)

The Difference Between Power and Authority

Let's fully examine verse 19 of Luke 10:

"I have given you...." **This is our promise**
It is not future; it is now. The original verb for "have given" is "dedocha." This verb is in the perfect tense—an action completed. It is not a future event; it is now true.

"I have given you authority..." **This is the gift of our promise**
The Greek word for "authority" is "exousia." It means "the right to act." The term here is applied to the seventy-two disciples.

"over all the power of the enemy..." **This is the object of our gift**
The Greek word for power is "dunamis." It means "might and ability." The term is applied here to Satan.

"Behold, I have given you authority (exousia) over all the power (dunamis) of the enemy."

Therefore, the believer has the right, or delegated authority, to act over ALL of the enemy's might and power through the name of Jesus Christ!

Many will argue that this authority was given only to the 72 that Jesus sent out and not to all believers. This is not so. We walk in kingdom authority as the children of God:

> **Ephesians 1:3** *Blessed be the God and Father of our Lord Jesus Christ, who has blessed us with every spiritual blessing in the heavenly places in Christ,*

> **Ephesians 1:11–12** *also we have obtained an inheritance, having been predestined according to His purpose who works all things after the counsel of His will, to the end that we who were the first to hope in Christ would be to the praise of His glory.*

> **Ephesians 2:19–22** *So then you are no longer strangers and aliens, but you are fellow citizens with the saints, and are of God's household, having been built on the foundation of the apostles and prophets, Christ Jesus Himself being the corner stone, in whom the whole building, being fitted together, is growing into a holy temple in the Lord, in whom you also are being built together into a dwelling of God in the Spirit.*

Our position in Christ as joint heirs and adopted children gives us the right to use the kingdom authority delegated to us as believers.

The enemy will oppose or come against the believer. But when he does, we have the full authority that Jesus delegated to us, in His name, over <u>all</u> the power that Satan or demons will bring against us.

The believer has many great promises, and also authority, at his disposal. This is part of knowing who you are in Christ Jesus. Being made complete in Christ, this authority is part of you as a new creation at the time of salvation, according to Colossians 2:10 (see below). As a believer, you are a joint heir with Christ, a co-worker with God, and a representative of His kingdom.

> **1 Corinthians 3:9** *For we are God's fellow workers; you are God's field, God's building.*

Luke 10:20 *"However, do not rejoice that the spirits submit to you, but rejoice that your names are written in heaven"*

We must not lose sight of the fact that having the ability to cast out demons is never proof that one is saved. We can conclude that since Judas was indeed one of the twelve, that he was just as successful in casting out demons as were the others (Luke 9:1–2). If he had been unable to do so, it would have caused Judas to "stand out amongst the other eleven" –something of which we have not even a hint in the Scriptures. In addition, the Lord's words in Matthew's gospel make it quite clear that unbelievers were able to cast out demons:

> **Matthew 7:22–23** *"Many will say to me on that day, 'Lord, Lord, did we not prophesy in your name, and in your name drive out demons and perform many miracles?' Then I will tell them plainly, 'I never knew you. Away from me, you evildoers!'"*

The authority of the name of Christ alone drives out demons. It is never about us or our own authority, but about the authority that resides in us since we are partakers with Christ.

Jesus told His disciples that rather than to rejoice that demons obey, they should rejoice in their salvation. They should take greater joy in the fact their names were written in heaven. At first, the disciples were caught up in their relationship with the spirit world; namely, that in Christ's name they had power over demons. Jesus told them that they should be rejoicing in their relationship with God!

I believe that the following verse is one of the most powerful verses in the Bible. Not only does it prove that Christ is God in the first half, but it truly defines a believer's position in Christ:

> **Colossians 2:9–10** *For in Him all the fullness of Deity dwells in bodily form, and in Him you have been made complete, and He is the head over all rule and authority;*

The previous verse allows one to understand why "greater is He that is in you, than He that is in the world."

1 John 4:4 *You are from God, little children, and have overcome them; because greater is He who is in you than he who is in the world.*

Remember, Satan has <u>no</u> authority over any child of God, unless that person gives up that authority to him. The next verses from Romans clearly show this:

Romans 6:12–14 *Therefore do not let sin reign in your mortal body so that you obey its lusts, and do not go on presenting the members of your body to sin as instruments of unrighteousness; but present yourselves to God as those alive from the dead, and your members as instruments of righteousness to God. For sin shall not be master over you, for you are not under law but under grace.*

Romans 6:16 *Do you not know that **when you present yourselves to someone as slaves for obedience, you are slaves of the one whom you obey**, either of sin resulting in death, or of obedience resulting in righteousness*

When a believer chooses to live in sin and not submit to God, he gives up his Christ-given authority to Satan.

When a believer lives in ignorance with regards to his position in Christ, he gives up his Christ-given authority to Satan.

When a believer chooses to believe the enemy's lies over the truth of what God has said, he gives up his Christ-given authority to Satan.

You must know God's Word, the truth, to be able to recognize a lie of Satan. Too many Christians base their life on feelings and emotions rather than truth. When one believes Satan over God, it is also a form of idolatry since you are trusting in something other than God.

If we know truth we cannot be taken captive:

Colossians 2:8 *See to it that no one takes you captive* *through philosophy and empty deception, according to the tradition of men, according to the elementary principles of the world, rather than according to Christ.*

Conclusion

As you can see, the believer and follower of Christ Jesus has full authority over the enemy. The believer's understanding of this authority is essential in the cosmic war. Knowing this, why would a believer lay down his authority, or allow demons to assert authority over him?

We are to occupy enemy territory as a soldier on duty in a defeated country. The believer's "country" is Heaven, since he is a citizen of Heaven.

Philippians 3:20 *For our citizenship is in heaven, from which also we eagerly wait for a Savior, the Lord Jesus Christ;*

The enemy's territory is this world. Our Lord has already defeated the enemy. So we are merely occupying the territory of the enemy.

No good soldier ever leaves or deserts his post. The Lord's soldiers are to be always on the watch and alert. The enemy is defeated; yet he is still present, and seeks to do guerilla warfare against the winning soldiers. When the enemy does, use your God-given position in Christ, stand, and overcome the enemy!

⁓ Chapter 7 ⁓

◆

Our Weapons of Warfare

"I have also had the opportunity to talk with some people who have gone through deliverance. It seems the enemy just wants to keep knocking them down, but we know different. I just give them the word in love and tell them it's so important to develop a relationship with Him alone. Just you and God. I remind them who they are in Him, and how important it is for them to know who they are as well. I stand on the word of God that says NO weapon formed against me shall prosper."

or though we walk in the flesh, we do not war according to the flesh, for the weapons of our warfare are not of the flesh, but divinely powerful for the destruction of fortresses. We are destroying speculations and every lofty thing raised up against the knowledge of God, and we are taking every thought captive to the obedience of Christ

-2 Corinthians 10:3–5

As you can see by the above Scripture verse, we have mighty weapons available to us. Satan's kingdom uses lies, speculations, and lofty ideas to take a believer captive. The believer who knows the truth can recognize these things and overcome the enemy. On this page we will look at some of our weapons of war. You must learn what these weapons are—and how to effectively use them—in order to have victory.

What Kind of Soldier is the Believer?

As a believer, you need to <u>know</u> who you are in Christ. You also must learn to see and accept yourself as God sees and accepts you. The next chart is a short list of terms that describe your new identity in Christ. See Appendix "A" for a more comprehensive list.

You Are...	Found In...
An Ambassador	2 Corinthians 5:20 & Ephesians 6:20
A New Creation	2 Corinthians 5:17
A Saint of God	1 Corinthians 1:2
An Heir of God	Galatians 3:29 & 4:7
Equipped for good work	2 Timothy 3:17
A Child of God	1 John 3:1
A Fellow Worker	1 Corinthians 3:9 & 2 Corinthians 6:1
Chosen of God	Ephesians 1:4 & Colossians 3:12
An Adopted Child	Ephesians 1:5
Alive in Christ	Ephesians 2:5

A Soldier	2 Timothy 2:3–4
A Holy Person, and part of a Holy Nation	1 Peter 2:9
Anointed	1 John 2:27
An Overcomer	1 John 5:4
A Son of God	Galatians 3:26
A Minister	1 Timothy 4:6
Reconciled to God	Colossians 1:22
A Conqueror	Romans 8:37
A Citizen	Philippians 3:20

All believers become all of these things at the time of their salvation. At that point, it is the birth of a *new* creation, having been born again. You weren't holy or a saint prior to your salvation, but you are afterward because you were born anew. Remember: these identity traits are all found in God's word, so they <u>are true</u> about you (whether you believe it or not)—because God said so!

Since you are in fact all these things now, then you should conduct yourself accordingly. Christ paid dearly to allow you to be all of this. So why would you dishonor Him by believing otherwise? Allow it to be lived out!

What the Enemy Doesn't Want You to Know!

You are no longer a sinner, a murderer, a fornicator, a liar, a cheater, or deserving of death, or separated from God, or an orphan. Nor are you condemned or guilty! These types of things are lies from the enemy to keep you a prisoner. Accepting these lies keeps you walking and acting outside of the true nature of a Child of God.

"Why or how can this be?" you may ask. When we come to Christ, having put our faith and trust in Him alone, we become born again. This process of being born again makes us new or changed, not merely "cleaned up."

2 Corinthians 5:17 *Therefore if anyone is in Christ, he is a new creature; the old things passed away; behold, new things have come.*

Colossians 3:10 *and have put on the new self who is being renewed to a true knowledge according to the image of the One who created him.*

When you become born again, you now take on the character and nature of Christ.

2 Peter 1:4 *For by these He has granted to us His precious and magnificent promises, so that by them you may become partakers of the divine nature, having escaped the corruption that is in the world by lust.*

Your old nature or character was crucified, and is **dead** and **buried** in Christ.

Romans 6:6 *knowing this, that our old self was crucified with Him, in order that our body of sin might be done away with, so that we would no longer be slaves to sin;*

Galatians 5:24 *Now those who belong to Christ Jesus have crucified the flesh with its passions and desires.*

Galatians 2:20 *I have been crucified with Christ; and it is no longer I who live, but Christ lives in me; and the life which I now live in the flesh I live by faith in the Son of God, who loved me and gave Himself up for me.*

This is the very key to walking in victory. You must learn, and know, and accept who you are as a believer. Agree with God! Walk in the character as you now are, not as you once were.

Our Armor is God; He is Our Divine Protection and Power

Ephesians 6:10 *Finally, be strong in the Lord and in the strength of His might.*

Power

"Be strong" means "to be empowered" or "having power from within." The way a believer gets power within is to be *"in the Lord"*. In other words, we get our defensive power by being in the Lord, or abiding in Him.

1 John 4:4 *You are from God, little children, and have overcome them; because greater is He [Holy Spirit] who is in you than he [Satan] who is in the world.*

Protection

He is our strong protection	2 Chronicles 16:9
He encamps about us	Psalm 34:7
He is like a fortress of high mountains	Psalm 125:2
He is like a wall of fire	Zechariah 2:5
He is our rear guard	Exodus 14:20
He is our defense	Psalm 5:11
He is our fortress	Psalm 144:2
He is our rock of defense	Psalm 18:2
He is our hiding place	Psalm 31:20
He is our place of refuge	Psalm 46:1
He is our shield	Psalm 84:11

The Armor that God Gives to Every Believer

Since we are made complete in Christ, who is ruler of all, the believer has all the armor he needs for occupying the enemy's territory.

Colossians 2:10 *and in Him you have been made complete, and He is the head over all rule and authority;*

As we look at this armor, understand that the armor is received, or put on the moment you become saved, and is never taken off, nor can it be since we are complete in Christ. Being complete in Christ means we lack nothing—ever. The translations say *"Put on,"* yet the correct translation is *"Having put on,"* an action completed. Nevertheless, with this armor we can stand firm against the enemy.

> **Ephesians 6:11–13** [Having]*put on the full armor of God, so that you will be able to stand firm against the schemes of the devil. For our struggle is not against flesh and blood, but against the rulers, against the powers, against the world forces of this darkness, against the spiritual forces of wickedness in the heavenly places. Therefore, take up the full armor of God, so that you will be able to resist in the evil day, and having done everything, to stand firm.*

The Specific Armor Listed in Verses 14 Through 18:

vs. 14

*"having girded your loins with **truth** "* – "Girded up" means "to bind, encircle, or to make oneself ready for." As we encircle ourselves with truth (God's Word), we can be prepared to move and function. This is protection for the believer's walk.

*"having put on the breastplate of **righteousness** "* – This refers to Jesus' righteousness in us. Feelings or emotions should not deceive the believer.

vs. 15

*"having shod your feet **with the preparation of the gospel of peace,"** which* actually means to be busy spreading the

Gospel, yet it is the same Gospel message that gives you the peace as well. Proper shoes are critical in war. The shoes of the believer are the peace of God that is achieved by knowing the Gospel.

vs. 16

*"in addition to all, taking up the shield of **faith** with which you will be able to extinguish all the flaming arrows of the evil one."* – The shield is also pictured as an "interlocking together" with other believers as we stand corporately as a church body. With the shield the believer can remain focused on who Christ is. This is the overall protection in Christ.

vs. 17

*"take the helmet of **salvation**"* – This is knowledge and assurance in Christ, and overall protection from evil thoughts and lies.

*"the sword of the Spirit, which is **the word of God**"* – Promises of God are written and guaranteed. With the Biblical truth of the Word of God, the believer can apply it to every situation.

vs. 18

*"With all **prayer and petition** pray at all times in the Spirit, and with this in view, be on the alert with all perseverance and petition for all the saints"* – Prayer is a call for defense and reliance on God. It keeps the believer connected to the source of power and might.

I might also add that the Word of God and prayer are the believer's only offensive weapons.

The Believer's Weapons

The Bible says that we have weapons, so what are they?

Weapon #1 - A Sword (The Word of God)

> **Ephesians 6:17** *"And take the helmet of salvation, and the* **sword** *of the Spirit, which is the* **word** *of God."*

The Word is listed as the major offensive weapon.

> **Revelation 19:15** *"From His mouth comes a sharp* **sword**, *so that with it He may strike down the nations, and He will rule them with a rod of iron; and He treads the wine press of the fierce wrath of God, the Almighty."*

> **Revelation 12:11** *"And they overcame him because of the blood of the Lamb and because of the* **word** *of their testimony, and they did not love their life even when faced with death."*

Jesus used the written Word against the devil, as a believer should:

> **Matthew 4:4** *But He answered and said, "It is written, 'Man shall not live on bread alone, but on every* **word** *that proceeds out of the mouth of God.'"*

Again in verses 7 and 10 of Matthew, Jesus said, *"it is written..."*

A believer needs to know and understand the Word of God and use it to expose lies, as well as to resist Satan and demons. This *Word* is Jesus and this is truth, therefore Jesus is the Sword. He is the source of the believer's authority and power.

Weapon #2 - Knowledge and Truth

Hosea 4:6 *"My people are destroyed for lack of knowledge. Because you have rejected knowledge, I also will reject you from being My priest. Since you have forgotten the law of your God, I also will forget your children."*

Ephesians 4:13 *"until we all reach unity in the faith and in the knowledge of the Son of God and become mature, attaining to the whole measure of the fullness of Christ."*

John 8:31–32 *"So Jesus was saying to those Jews who had believed Him, 'If you continue in My word, then you are truly disciples of Mine; and you will know the truth, and the truth will make you free.'"*

A believer's walk with God is to be based on truth, <u>not on feelings or emotions</u>. The written promises and truths of God should be applied to every situation in order to put out the lies and flaming arrows of deception from the evil one. If one does not know truth, then one cannot recognize lies. Lies are the enemy's native language.

Weapon #3 - Faith

You can only do spiritual warfare if you have faith:

Matthew 17:19–20 *"Then the disciples came to Jesus privately and said, 'Why could we not drive it out?' And He said to them, 'Because of the littleness of your **faith**; for truly I say to you, if you have **faith** the size of a mustard seed, you will say to this mountain, 'Move from here to there' and it will move; and nothing will be impossible to you.'"*

Matthew 21:21–22 *And Jesus answered and said to them, "Truly I say to you, **if you have faith and do not doubt**, you*

*will not only do what was done to the fig tree, but even if
you say to this mountain, 'Be taken up and cast into the
sea,' it will happen. And all things you ask in prayer,
believing, you will receive."*

Faith is also the believer's shield against the enemy.

Ephesians 6:16 *in addition to all, taking up the **shield of
faith** with which you will be able to extinguish all the
flaming arrows of the evil one.*

The believer must walk in faith:
* Faith in God's character
* Faith in God's Word
* Faith in your identity in Christ

Weapon #4 - The Authority of the Name of Jesus Christ

John 16:26 *"In that day you will ask in **My name**, and I
do not say to you that I will request of the Father on your
behalf;*

Acts 16:18 *She continued doing this for many days. But
Paul was greatly annoyed, and turned and said to the
spirit, "I command you **in the name of Jesus Christ** to
come out of her!" And it came out at that very moment.*

Weapon #5 - A Life Submitted to God

Romans 12:1–2 *"Therefore I urge you, brethren, by the
mercies of God, to present your bodies a living and holy
sacrifice, acceptable to God, which is your spiritual service
of worship. And do not be conformed to this world, but be
transformed by the renewing of your mind, so that you may
prove what the will of God is, that which is good and
acceptable and perfect."*

2 Timothy 2:4 *"No soldier in active service entangles himself in the affairs of everyday life, so that he may please the one who enlisted him as a soldier."*

James 4:7 *"Submit therefore to God. Resist the devil and he will flee from you."*

1 John 5:18 *"We know that no one who is born of God sins; but He who was born of God keeps him, and the evil one does not touch him."*

The believer's life must be submitted to God and abiding in God. When a believer is in line with God by agreeing with Him, that believer is under God's divine protection.
However, if a believer walks in *continual* disobedience, that believer opens himself to demonic attack as open game, and hunting season begins on his or her life!

Deuteronomy 28:7 *The LORD shall cause your enemies who rise up against you to be defeated before you; they will come out against you one way and will flee before you seven ways.*

The believer who has an awareness and understanding of these weapons doesn't need to be taken into captivity by the enemy. Your armor enables you to live and survive in this defeated territory. The armor is failsafe, since it is empowered by the Lord.
Now that you know this truth, use your God-given weapons! Again, believers have these weapons and armor at the moment of salvation. Weapons are only good to a soldier if he has an understanding of their proper use and power. If not, he is only carrying dead weight.
Unfortunately, many believers today are either unaware of them or lack understanding about them. They become war casualties.

Chapter 8

◆

Being Victorious

"I just say the Scriptures and know that they are real. Not that I ever doubted them, just that things are different now. Things that used to move me don't anymore; I don't get angry and frustrated. I just relax and trust God. I know who I am."

A majority of believers experience "down times" in their Christian walk. This is a normal occurrence. God often uses times like these to grow us. However, when these "down times" persist over long periods, the believer can be rendered useless and begin to feel crippled. A believer will usually realize that something is wrong with him, but seldom few suspect demonization. Many are sincere, Spirit-filled Christians who truly love God, but are often bound by unexplainable fears, confusion, uncontrollable emotions, sinful habits, and other addictions and bondages. In Chapter 13 we will see how to become free from all this and more.

How do we STAY free from becoming demonized, either after salvation or after being freed through deliverance? It's all about issues of the flesh and mind!

Submitting to the Lordship of Christ

Central to all sin is the failure to love God fully and to submit ourselves in obedience to His divine will and purpose for our lives. Failure to submit to God is to side with Satan's kingdom in adopting the view that we know better than God, and therefore we will decide for ourselves how to live our lives. Choosing Satan's side in the ongoing cosmic war between good and evil will put one at risk of coming under the control of Satan's demonic angels.

> **James 4:7** *Submit therefore to God. Resist the devil and he will flee from you.*

Submitting is the very key in having victory over sin and demons. Total submission to the Lordship of Jesus Christ means giving your whole self: flesh (body), soul (mind, will, and emotions), and spirit (the new creation). Not just parts; or some; or most…but **all** of you! You need to be dead to yourself and let Christ live through you.

When you are in full submission to God, you are under His protection (1 John 5:18). You *can be protected* from demonization and from acting on sin. Once you act independently of God, though, you are open game for demon attack!

Colossians 3:1–10 *Therefore if you have been raised up with Christ, keep seeking the things above, where Christ is, seated at the right hand of God. Set your mind on the things above, not on the things that are on earth. For you have died and your life is hidden with Christ in God. When Christ, who is our life, is revealed, then you also will be revealed with Him in glory. Therefore consider the members of your earthly body as dead to immorality, impurity, passion, evil desire, and greed, which amounts to idolatry. For it is because of these things that the wrath of God will come upon the sons of disobedience, and in them you also once walked, when you were living in them. But now you also, put them all aside: anger, wrath, malice, slander, and abusive speech from your mouth. Do not lie to one another, since you laid aside the old self with its evil practices, and have put on the new self who is being renewed to a true knowledge according to the image of the One who created him.*

The Flesh

The Flesh (that which your spirit person dwells in) is sinful. As a believer, we are to walk in the spirit and not walk in the flesh.

Galatians 5:16–17 *But I say, walk by the Spirit, and you will not carry out the desire of the flesh. For the flesh sets its desire against the Spirit, and the Spirit against the flesh; for these are in opposition to one another, so that you may not do the things that you please.*

What are the deeds or evidence of the flesh?

Galatians 5:19–21 *Now the deeds of the flesh are evident, which are: immorality, impurity, sensuality, idolatry, sorcery, enmities, strife, jealousy, outbursts of anger, disputes, dissensions, factions, envying, drunkenness, carousing, and things like these, of which I forewarn you, just as I have forewarned you, that those who practice such* *things will not inherit the kingdom of God.*

The "flesh" is the tendency within every person to operate independently of God, and to center your interests on yourself—a form of idolatry and pride.

What are the deeds or evidence of the Spirit?

> **Galatians 5:22–24** *But the fruit of the Spirit is love, joy, peace, patience, kindness, goodness, faithfulness, gentleness, self-control; against such things there is no law. Now those who belong to Christ Jesus have crucified the flesh with its passions and desires.*

These are produced only as you yield and submit to God. They are not produced of your own accord. They are fruits of the Spirit, not of your life.

As a believer we *used* to walk in the flesh and the character of the flesh. But now we are to walk in the character of God. This is done by renewing your mind. The word "renew" means "to change one's perspective or outlook."

> **Ephesians 4:17–24** *So this I say, and affirm together with the Lord, that **you walk no longer** just as the Gentiles also walk, in the futility of their mind, being darkened in their understanding, excluded from the life of God because of the ignorance that is in them, because of the hardness of their heart; and they, having become callous, have given themselves over to sensuality for the practice of every kind of impurity with greediness. But you did not learn Christ in this way, if indeed you have heard Him and have been taught in Him, just as truth is in Jesus, that, in reference to your former manner of life, **you lay aside the old self**, which is being corrupted in accordance with the lusts of deceit, and that you be **renewed in the spirit of your mind**, and **put on the new self**, which in the likeness of God has been created in righteousness and holiness of the truth.*

> **Ephesians 5:8–11** *for **you were formerly darkness**, but now you are Light in the Lord; **walk as children of Light***

(for the fruit of the Light consists in all goodness and righteousness and truth), trying to learn what is pleasing to the Lord. Do not participate in the unfruitful deeds of darkness, but instead even expose them;

You change or renew your mind by seeing things God's way. His perspective must become your perspective. Again, this also is part of submitting to God. When we live according to the flesh it is because we have our minds set on the flesh.

Romans 8:5–8 *For those who are according to the flesh set their minds on the things of the flesh, but those who are according to the Spirit, the things of the Spirit. For the mind set on the flesh is death, but the mind set on the Spirit is life and peace, because the mind set on the flesh is hostile toward God; for it does not subject itself to the law of God, for it is not even able to do so, and those who are in the flesh cannot please God.*

We are not under any obligation to live by the flesh.

Romans 8:12 *So then, brethren, we are under obligation, not to the flesh, to live according to the flesh*

We are to be dead to sin. Sin is no longer the master of your life as it was when you did not have Christ. Jesus Christ is to be your only master.

Romans 6:11–17 *Even so consider yourselves to be dead to sin, but alive to God in Christ Jesus. Therefore do not let sin reign in your mortal body so that you obey its lusts, and do not go on presenting the members of your body to sin as instruments of unrighteousness; but present yourselves to God as those alive from the dead, and your members as instruments of righteousness to God. For sin shall not be master over you, for you are not under law but under grace. What then? Shall we sin because we are not under law but under grace? May it never be! Do you not know that when you present yourselves to someone as* *slaves for obedience, you are slaves of the one whom you obey, either of sin resulting in death, or of obedience resulting in righteousness? But thanks be to God that though you were slaves of sin, you became obedient from the heart to that form of teaching to which you were committed,*

You are called to walk in a manner worthy of your calling. Even though you still live in the sin-filled body, you no longer need to walk in the ways of sin. Your spirit man is to be submitted to God, not submitted to or enslaved by the flesh. You do not have to obey the flesh any more. It is not who you are!

Let's look at a story from the world's point of view:

If your father was the ruler of the greatest kingdom on earth, that would make you a child of the king, right? You would dress and act a certain way. You would walk in power because of the authority that your father had delegated to you. People of the kingdom would recognize you as the child of the king. It is the character of who you are, since it is also your father's character you represent.

Would you, then, as a child of the king, walk around the kingdom dressed and acting like the regular people? No, of course not! Why? Because that's not who you are! You would be acting out of character if you did.

It is no different in the spiritual kingdom. You are a child of the Most High King! You have been given the Holy Spirit and you represent the Father's Kingdom. So why would you act like the heathen of the world? You no longer need to; you are born again into the Kingdom of God. So walk in the character of who you are now, not as you once were.

Live for the will of God!

1 Peter 4:2–3 *so as to live the rest of the time in the flesh* **no longer for the lusts of men, but for the will of God.** *For the time already past is sufficient for you to have* *carried out the desire of the Gentiles, having pursued a course of sensuality, lusts, drunkenness, carousing, drinking parties and abominable idolatries.*

When we live in the flesh we make a provision or an opportunity for Satan and his demons to use.

Ephesians 4:27 *and do not give the devil an opportunity.*

We should be self-controlled. Control your flesh and it's desires through the power of God.

1 Peter 5:8 *Be self-controlled and alert. Your enemy the devil prowls around like a roaring lion looking for someone to devour.* (NIV)

Guarding the Mind

We are also continually warned in Scripture with regards to our mind and thoughts. We are told to fix our minds and thoughts on God and above. We are supposed to renew and transform our minds and ways of thinking, not to think on the sinful things we used to do and be. If a believer does not learn the way to victory in the war for his mind and thoughts, he will begin to form the evil habits of vain imagination and fantasies. He will begin to lose control over his thoughts and emotions.

2 Corinthians 10:3–5 addresses this: *"For though we live in the world, we do not...We demolish arguments and every pretension that sets itself up against the knowledge of God, and we take captive every thought to make it obedient to Christ."* (NIV)

Romans 12:2 *And do not be conformed to this world, but be transformed by the renewing of your mind, so that you may prove what the will of God is, that which is good and acceptable and perfect.*

Ephesians 4:23 *and that you be renewed in the spirit of your mind,*

The mind is where the main battle goes on between your life in God, the thoughts of your flesh, and outside thoughts placed there by the demonic world. If you do not submit your thoughts to a Christ-like mind, you will give into temptations, fall into sin, and break fellowship with God, thus losing His protection (not losing salvation). This will open you up for demonization, and provide a way for you to be led into captivity to do Satan's will in your life (2 Timothy 2:25–26).

True knowledge for the mind comes from God and His Word. All other wisdom and thinking is worldly and of the devil, as the book of James addresses in the following passage:

James 3:13–18 *Who among you is wise and understanding? Let him show by his good behavior his deeds in the gentleness of wisdom. But if you have bitter jealousy and selfish ambition in your heart, do not be arrogant and so lie against the truth. <u>This wisdom is not that which comes down from above, but is earthly, natural, demonic.</u> For where jealousy and selfish ambition exist, there is disorder and every evil thing. But the wisdom from above is first pure, then peaceable, gentle, reasonable, full of mercy and good fruits, unwavering, without hypocrisy. And the seed whose fruit is righteousness is sown in peace by those who make peace.*

Conclusion

In order to remain victorious in your Christian walk,

1) Submit to the Lordship of Jesus
2) Walk in the Spirit
3) Guard your mind

When you learn to walk by the Spirit of God and not by the flesh or earthly wisdom, then you walk in truth. Jesus said, "Then you will know the truth, and the truth will set you free" (John 8:32). When you begin to understand your true character and the fact that you now have the nature of Christ in you, then it will be easier for you to enslave your mind and flesh to God instead of the world or the evil ones. You will walk in the character of who you are now as a New Creation. You will be conforming to the image of Christ. This is a vital key to walking in victory rather than defeat.

Chapter 9

◆

Concerning Prayers

"My faith has increased, as well as my confidence, since understanding your teaching on prayer through the online counseling. I no longer have doubts or double-mindedness. There is a sense of peace."

There are two questions that I am asked regularly:

- "Why are my prayers not answered?"
- "How do I have my prayers answered?"

These are normal questions. The Word of God guides us to the answers. Let's see what the Bible says about four main reasons for unanswered prayer.

1) Sin & Lack of Obedience

When a believer sins or lives in sin, fellowship with God is broken (not salvation). When you are out of fellowship, God cannot bless you, nor does He honor your prayers. The only prayer He will honor when you are out of His will, and thus His fellowship, is the prayer of confession. Let's look at Scripture to support this statement:

> **1 Peter 3:12** *For the eyes of the Lord are on the righteous and his ears are attentive to their prayer, but the face of the Lord is against those who do evil.* (NIV)

Note that the verse above was written to believers in the church.

Also in the Bible, God says, *"and if My people, who are called by My name, humble themselves and pray and seek My face and turn from their wicked ways, then I will hear from heaven, will forgive their sin and will heal their land."* (2 Chronicles 7:14)

A believer should not think for one minute that he can walk continually in sin and disobedience and expect a Holy God to respond to his prayer requests. If there is willful sin in your life, be sure to repent and change your mind. Turn to God and allow His forgiveness to be applied and restore fellowship. If you find your prayers are not getting answered, it may be because there is sin in your walk with God.

2) Doubt & Lack of Faith

A believer should not doubt when praying. Believers must believe in God and His divine will and promises.

> **James 1:6–8** *But he must ask in faith without any doubting, for the one who <u>doubts</u> is like the surf of the sea, driven and tossed by the wind. For that man <u>ought not to expect that he will receive anything from the Lord</u>, being a double-minded man, unstable in all his ways.*

Doubt is the opposite of faith. Doubt is to have faith in what the enemy says and not what God has said. The Bible clearly says you shall have whatever it is you say. If you are in line with God, His will, and what He says, then you are in line for answered prayer. However, if you have faith in the words or thoughts of doubt, you shall also receive accordingly.

Everyone at one time or another experiences doubt. When there is doubt, learn to come to God and give Him that doubt as well.

3) Unforgiveness

Forgiveness is an attitude of one's heart. It is the power of the Holy Spirit that enables a believer to forgive. The following Scripture verse shows why it is important to forgive others before you can approach God in prayer:

> **Matthew 6:14–15** *For if you forgive others for their transgressions, your heavenly Father will also forgive you. But if you do not forgive others, then your Father will not forgive your transgressions.*

John Maxwell writes in his book, *Partners in Prayer:*

> "Forgiving and being forgiven are inseparable twins. When a person refuses to forgive another, he is hurting himself, because his lack of forgiveness can take hold of

him and make him bitter. And a person cannot enter prayer with bitterness and come out with blessings. Forgiveness allows your heart to be made not only right, but light." [5]

4) God's Perfect Will and Timing

There will also be times of unanswered prayer even if the previously mentioned conditions and principles are met. This is because God has a perfect will and perfect timing. He knows *what* you need—and *when* you need it—even if you do not. He is in control and knows all things. His divine will must always come before your self-wants and desires. A believer's purpose in life is to glorify God.

> **Ephesians 1:11** *also we have obtained an inheritance, having been predestined according to His purpose who works all things after the counsel of His will,*
>
> **Matthew 6:8** *"So do not be like them; for your Father knows what you need before you ask Him.*
>
> **Philippians 2:13** *for it is God who is at work in you, both to will and to work for His good pleasure.*
>
> **Romans 8:26** *In the same way the Spirit also helps our weakness; for we do not know how to pray as we should, but the Spirit Himself intercedes for us with groanings too deep for words;*

There are even more reasons as to why prayers go unanswered, such as: wrong motives and an unsurrendered will. I would like to suggest for further study on prayer, read John Maxwell's *Partners in Prayer*, published by Thomas Nelson, 1996.

How to Be Assured of Answered Prayer

The key to having prayers answered is abiding in Christ: not partially, but fully. This is the same as submitting fully to God as discussed in the chapter 8, "Being Victorious." The Bible says that we can have confidence in prayer:

> **1 John 3:21–22** *Beloved, if our heart does not condemn us, we have confidence before God; and whatever we ask we receive from Him,* ***because*** *we keep His commandments and do the things that are pleasing in His sight.*

When a believer has sin or doubt ruling in their life, there is no way to have this kind of confidence. But when abiding with God, the confidence is indeed there—along with assurance and peace. If you desire to do spiritual warfare, you will need to have this confidence and assurance during battles. If not, the enemy will overtake you in a heartbeat.

Once you have submitted to the previous criteria, you can follow the Biblical outline below for being on praying grounds. But you should prepare your heart before praying.

> **Psalm 46:10** *Be still, and know that I am God; I will be exalted among the nations, I will be exalted in the earth.*
> (NIV)

Pray intelligently, and with a purpose. Do this in correct fellowship with the Lord by following these four aspects of a prayer model:

1) <u>Adoration</u> - Enter into correct fellowship with God with respect and adoration. This is a time to reflect on His attributes, such as His greatness, power, mercy, majesty, and grace.

2) <u>Confession</u> - When you come into God's presence, He will convict you of sin. This is a time for restoring fellowship through repentance. Apply His forgiveness to your sins.

3) <u>Thanksgiving</u> - Spend time thanking God for His mercies, grace and love. Thank Him for the blessings and works done in your life.

4) <u>Supplication</u> - Now is the correct time to make your needs or requests known to God.

Using the previous outline, here is a short example of a prayer encompassing the 4 aspects:

> Father God, you alone are great and holy. Lord, you are full of mercy and grace. Your love and power is unlimited. You alone are God!

> Father, I confess to you that I have sinned against you today. I agree with you and repent of these things. I told a lie today to my friend. Lord, I also stole time from my employer. I clocked in early, but I did not begin to work for 20 minutes. Lord, I will also confess to my boss and make restitution by offering 30 minutes of work off the clock. I will also confess my lie to my friend. Please have mercy! I receive your forgiveness and ask for our fellowship to be restored in the power of the Holy Spirit.

> Thank you father, for your grace and mercy. I thank you that you love me beyond measure.

> Lord God, I ask now for the needs of my friends to be met according to your will. I also ask for wisdom to be a stronger and bolder witness for your kingdom. Lord Jesus, I also ask for protection for my family. Please, Lord, keep the evil ones from my family. Bless our church and fellowship, and guide me by your right hand. In Jesus name I ask, amen.

Now, pray in power, faith, and assurance. Boldly and confidently pray as you stand on praying grounds.

Chapter 10

♦

A Word on Angels

"Bill, when you prayed for me the other night during the battle, I sensed a peace. During the deliverance when the demon of Anger was manifesting, you asked God to surround us with war angels. There was a release...my throat was somehow being choked and then it stopped!"

The term "angel," in both the Hebrew and Greek languages, means "messenger." In this chapter, we will look at some truth from God's Word about angels.

First, let me say that angels and demons are eternal beings and cannot die. God created angels to do His bidding and carry out His divine plans. They are also ministers of God's goodness to believers. They carry out God's judgments as well. They fight against demons for the glory of God and also do so on behalf of the believer.

Since angels and demons are eternal and cannot die, they can only advance or retreat (in addition, demons can be sent to the abyss—see Luke 8:31). When God's people fail to pray and abide in God, demons are allowed to advance and get the upper hand; however, when God's people pray, angels are sent in to demolish demonic strongholds and drive back the demons (refer to Daniel chapter 10 to see a picture of this).

What are Angels, and What Do They Do?

1. **Angels are spiritual beings created by God.**

   Genesis 1:1 *In the beginning God created the heavens and the earth.*

   Nehemiah 9:6 *You alone are the LORD. You have made the heavens, the heaven of heavens with all their host, the earth and all that is on it, the seas and all that is in them. You give life to all of them and the heavenly host bows down before You.*

   Colossians 1:16–17 *For by Him all things were created, both in the heavens and on earth, visible and invisible, whether thrones or dominions or rulers or authorities—all things have been created through Him and for Him. He is before all things, and in Him all things hold together.*

2. **Angels have considerable power, but only God is all-powerful.**

Psalm 103:20 *Bless the LORD, you His angels, mighty in strength, who perform His word, obeying the voice of His word!*

2 Kings 19:35 *Then it happened that night that the angel of the LORD went out and struck 185,000 in the camp of the Assyrians; and when the men rose early in the morning, behold, all of them were dead.*

Matthew 28:2 *And behold, a severe earthquake had occurred, for an* **angel** *of the Lord descended from heaven and came and* **rolled away** *the* **stone** *and sat upon it.*

3. **Angels do war for God.**

   2 Kings 6:17 *Then Elisha prayed and said, "O LORD, I pray, open his eyes that he may see." And the LORD opened the servant's eyes and he saw; and behold, the mountain was full of horses and chariots of fire all around Elisha.*

   Revelation 12:7 *And there was war in heaven, Michael and his angels waging war with the dragon. The dragon and his angels waged war,*

4. **Angels sometimes carry out God's judgment.**

   Matthew 13:49–50 *"So it will be at the end of the age; the angels will come forth and take out the wicked from among the righteous, and will throw them into the furnace of fire; in that place there will be weeping and gnashing of teeth."*

5. **Angels care for children and the outcast.**

   Matthew 18:10 *See that you do not despise one of these little ones, for I say to you that their angels in heaven continually* *see the face of My Father who is in heaven.*

6. Angels deliver messages from God to men.

Matthew 1:20 *But when he had considered this, behold, an angel of the Lord appeared to him in a dream, saying, "Joseph, son of David, do not be afraid to take Mary as your wife; for the Child who has been conceived in her is of the Holy Spirit."*

Acts 27:23–24 *For this very night an angel of the God to whom I belong and whom I serve stood before me, saying, "Do not be afraid, Paul; you must stand before Caesar; and behold, God has granted you all those who are sailing with you."*

7. Angels will return with Jesus.

Matthew 25:31 *"But when the Son of Man comes in His glory, and all the angels with Him, then He will sit on His glorious throne."*

8. Angels worship God in heaven.

Revelation 5:11–12 *Then I looked, and I heard the voice of many angels around the throne and the living creatures and the elders; and the number of them was myriads of myriads, and thousands of thousands, saying with a loud voice, "Worthy is the Lamb that was slain to receive power and riches and wisdom and might and honor and glory and blessing."*

9. Angels engage in spiritual warfare on behalf of believers.

In the following passage, Gabriel, a high-ranking angel, speaks to Daniel:

Daniel 10:10–21 *Then behold, a hand touched me and set* *me trembling on my hands and knees. He said to me, "O Daniel, man of high esteem, understand the words that I am about to tell you and stand upright, for I have now been sent to you." And when he had spoken this word to me, I stood up trembling.*

Then he said to me, "Do not be afraid, Daniel, for from the first day that you set your heart on understanding this and on humbling yourself before your God, your words were heard, and I have come in response to your words. But the prince of the kingdom of Persia **[A high ranking Demon Principality]** *was withstanding me for twenty-one days; then behold, Michael, one of the chief princes* **[A high-ranking Angel]**, *came to help me, for I had been left there with the kings of Persia* **[Demon Rulers in high places]**. *Now I have come to give you an understanding of what will happen to your people in the latter days, for the vision pertains to the days yet future."*

When he had spoken to me according to these words, I turned my face toward the ground and became speechless. And behold, one who resembled a human being was touching my lips; then I opened my mouth and spoke and said to him who was standing before me, "O my lord, as a result of the vision anguish has come upon me, and I have retained no strength. For how can such a servant of my lord talk with such as my lord? As for me, there remains just now no strength in me, nor has any breath been left in me."

Then this one with human appearance touched me again and strengthened me. He said, "O man of high esteem, do not be afraid. Peace be with you; take courage and be courageous!"

Now as soon as he spoke to me, I received strength and said, "May my lord speak, for you have strengthened me."

Then he said, "Do you understand why I came to you? But I shall now return to fight against the prince of Persia **[High-ranking Demon Principality]**; *so I am going forth, and behold, the prince of Greece* **[Another high-ranking Demon Principality coming to assist in the**

battle] *is about to come. However, I will tell you what is inscribed in the writing of truth. Yet there is no one who stands firmly with me against these forces except Michael your prince* **[Chief ruling Angel for the Jewish nation]**...*"*

When ministering to a demonized believer, I often ask God to send holy angels to assist in the deliverance. On numerous occasions when a demon is manifesting and being stubborn, I ask God to have an angel smite the demon. Once that is done, I have witnessed that the demon will cooperate. I have also asked God to allow an angel to administer love and peace to the demonized person and have gotten reactions ranging from agony to a feeling of peace.

We are in no way ever to glorify or worship an angel. We are in the war together with the angels and serve the same King: Jesus Christ. Angels are sent as ministering spirits to assist those that are to inherit the Kingdom of God (the believer in Jesus). They war against the demonic world all day long and fight with us, and for us. They are available to the believer in Christ, so trust God to send them (2 Kings 6:16–17). Never depend on them or glorify them in any way. All believers are to depend on God and worship God alone, as the angels do. God will deploy angels as He sees fit.

Chapter 11

♦

Curses?

"I never realized until now that some of the sin patterns in my life were the same as the ones my parents struggled with. I just want to be free of all this junk, and to be able to live a victorious overcoming life. I appreciate you taking the time to help me, I really do."

$\mathcal{T}$he subject of curses is often neglected in churches and Bible studies. Yet God has much to say about them in His Word. Believers must realize that we do live in a sin-cursed world. There are cursed people all around us. Satan and his demons thrive on curses, and God uses these spirits to carry them out on sinners.

A Sin Pattern or a Curse?

I have included this chapter as a very important part of spiritual warfare teaching. Most of the believers I minister to have some form of a sin pattern following them. A sin pattern is a genetic weakness in the flesh that occurs in some or all of the people in a particular family. Many ministers claim these sin patterns are "a curse." The Bible does not use the word "curse"; but "iniquity," or sin:

> **Exodus 20:5–6** *You shall not worship them or serve them; for I, the Lord your God, am a jealous God, visiting the <u>iniquity of the fathers on the children</u>, on the third and the fourth generations of those who hate Me, but showing loving kindness to thousands, to those who love Me and keep My commandments.*

> **Jeremiah 32:18** *who shows loving kindness to thousands, but repays the <u>iniquity of fathers into the bosom of their children after them</u>, O great and mighty God. The Lord of hosts is His name;*

> **Numbers 14:18** *The Lord is slow to anger and abundant in loving kindness, forgiving iniquity and transgression; but He will by no means clear the guilty, <u>visiting the iniquity of the fathers on the children</u> to the third and the fourth generations.*

Generational Sins

Generational sins are patterns that bring about strongholds in a family because of sins perpetuated by family members in a number of generations. This pattern is carried out through the nature of the flesh. This sin pattern brings about bondage to the same sins as the parents. This bondage will occur during an individual's life, until that individual addresses the sin issues that had put the sin into effect.

Generational sins are some of the biggest demonic strongholds in a person's life. Most do not even recognize it as a pattern that was passed down, but just "something they live with." When parents sin against God and follow the occult, false religions, and secret societies such as Freemasonry or The Illuminati—besides their personal sins—, the children are the ones who suffer.

Many children are born with this sin pattern that indwells a child's flesh. Demons are opportunists. They wait for the child to act out on any of these sin patterns, thereby making a provision in the flesh. Once that sin begins, it becomes an open door for demons to use to take them into bondage. This type of sin and bondage is easily recognized when you see the children carrying out the same sins of one or more of their parents or grandparents.

Examples of this type of sin pattern are listed below:

1) If a parent smokes and is addicted to smoking, one or more of the children may also be addicted.

2) If there is homosexuality in the family line, one or more of the children may be a homosexual.

3) If there is divorce in the family, one or more of the children may seek divorce when they become married, and may repeat it several times.

4) If depression and suicide are in the family line, one or more of the children may struggle with the same (and even more mental issues).

5) If sexual molestation or perversion is in the family line, one or more of the children may engage in, or be victims of, it over and over again as they grow up, by many different abusers.

These are but a few. We definitely can inherit spiritual sin patterns from our forefathers because of their sin and disobedience to God. I wanted to settle this in your mind and clear your understanding; that what many are preaching as a "curse" is actually sin.

Now you must understand that at salvation, one becomes a new creation and is made complete in Christ. At the time of new birth, the believer is set free from sin and demons in an instant. The demons that were attached to any sin patterns being passed down are immediately cast out, along with any other demons.

However, they do lie in wait for an open door of sin so that they can come back in through the genetic weakness, or sin code, that is still a part of the flesh body of the new believer.

Think of this sin code as a predisposition toward particular sin issues. If left undiscipled in truth, the new believer may, out of ignorance, open himself up to this besetting generational sin. Once the new believer chooses to sin in this area continually, the demons move back in and take up dominion. The new believer then continues in the struggle and defeat of the sin pattern passed down, until they choose to repent of it and deal with it. The believer must see it for what it is and seek freedom from it.

What are curses?

We have just seen that there is a distinction between "sin patterns" (iniquity) and "curses." So what is a curse?

- *A curse spoken by God* is for judgment or chastisement as a result of disobedience and sin. This may be personal, national, or generational, as seen in the Old Testament. However, God never curses believers—His own children in Christ! Why did God curse people (even the Israelites) in the Old Testament, but not believers in the New Testament? Because we are not under the law but under grace. Jesus took the curse upon the cross. The Old Testament people were not the holy temple of God, with God living inside, as we are today. This is why you do not find God cursing anyone in the New Testament.

- *A curse spoken by a person* (such as a witch) is a wish for harm to come to someone or something.

Where Do Curses Come From?

The answer may startle you…but they are from God! God is the one who set forth blessings and curses before all people.

> **Deuteronomy 11:26–28** *See, I am setting before you today a blessing and a curse: the blessing, if you listen to the commandments of the LORD your God, which I am commanding you today; and the curse, if you do not listen to the commandments of the LORD your God, but turn aside from the way which I am commanding you today, by following other gods which you have not known.*

Does a Believer Need to Fear a Curse?

The subject of dealing with curses has generally been neglected and hidden from the Body of Christ. While various religions around the world are professionals at using curses against the people of God (such as witchcraft, voodoo, tribal witchdoctors and medicine men, etc.), most believers are ignorant of how to deal with curses. All this despite the fact that Jesus clearly enabled us to do so!

A curse can never affect a believer since Jesus hung on the tree (cross) to free us from the curses. He became a curse for every man, to redeem us from the curse of the law:

> **Galatians 3:13** *Christ redeemed us from the curse of the Law, having become a curse for us—for it is written, "CURSED IS EVERYONE WHO HANGS ON A TREE"*

God's provision for His people is great! We should be focused on our God, who is our source of strength, provisions, and protection. Fearing Satan, his demons, and/or curses only gives the enemy more power over our life.

Fear is not trusting God or not agreeing with Him. The believer who fears is really yielding to the lies and intimidations of the enemy. The truth will set people free (John 8:32). Believing or agreeing with the enemy's lies keeps us in bondage. A curse cannot affect a believer—including ones spoken by a witch—unless the believer allows the fear of it to take hold. The curse does not have the power, but the sin of believing the curse over God does. Followers of Christ must live by the truth of God and His Word. The believer has no need to fear a curse *if they abide in God and His words.*

> **Numbers 22:12** *God said to Balaam, "Do not go with them; you shall not curse the people, for they are blessed."*

> **Deuteronomy 23:5** *Nevertheless, the LORD your God was not willing to listen to Balaam, but the LORD your God turned the curse into a blessing for you because the LORD your God loves you.*

God's protection is in place for a believer who is abiding in the Lord. He will not allow a curse to land upon a believer's life.

> **Proverbs 26:2** *Like a fluttering sparrow or a darting swallow, an undeserved curse does not come to rest.* (NIV)

Curses *are* in effect against unbelievers (both national and personal) because of sin and disobedience.

> **Malachi 2:2** *"If you do not listen, and if you do not take it to heart to give honor to My name," says the LORD of hosts, "then I will send the curse upon you and I will curse your blessings; and indeed, I have cursed them already, because you are not taking it to heart."*

> **Psalm 119:21** *You rebuke the arrogant, the cursed, who wander from Your commandments.*

> **Jeremiah 17:5–7** *Thus says the Lord, "Cursed is the man who trusts in mankind and makes flesh his strength, and*

*whose heart turns away from the Lord. For he will be like
a bush in the desert and will not see when prosperity
comes, but will live in stony wastes in the wilderness, a
land of salt without inhabitant. Blessed is the man who
trusts in the Lord and whose trust is the Lord."*

The believer whose trust is in the Lord is blessed and not
cursed! Praise the Lord! However, also be aware that God will
discipline His children who live in sin.

Hebrews 12:7–8 *It is for discipline that you endure; God
deals with you as with sons; for what son is there whom his
father does not discipline? But if you are without
discipline, of which all have become partakers, then you
are illegitimate children and not sons.*

Curses Spoken from Our Lips

Even believers can speak evil from their own lips against
themselves or others. To speak a curse is to wish evil intent or
harm on someone. Words spoken with lies and hatred invoke ill
will. You can curse yourself by speaking the lies of the enemy,
such as saying you are unworthy or rejecting yourself out loud. To
say the words "I'm a failure" is to curse yourself. In fact, as a
believer you are not receiving a curse; but rather, believing a lie.

Christians would be appalled to know that they have
pronounced curses by wishing and speaking out loud that others—
or themselves—were dead. When a person says, "damn you" or
"damn that …," they are pronouncing curses!

James 3:8–10 *But no one can tame the tongue; it is a
restless evil and full of deadly poison. With it we bless our
Lord and Father, and with it we curse men, who have been
made in the likeness of God; from the same mouth come
both blessing and cursing. My brethren, these things ought
not to be this way.*

Proverbs 18:21 *Death and life are in the power of the*

tongue, and those who love it will eat its fruit.

Words Spoken By Others

Since blessings and curses are a very real part of God's spiritual laws and principles, many use it to their sinful gain. Witches have long known the power of spoken words that the church is ignorant about. Sinful people may speak powerful things that they do not even understand that may affect the lives of others. We are to be aware of the words we speak and to whom we speak them.

Have you noticed that when a parent says to a child, "You are stupid and will never amount to anything!" the child usually grows up living that out? Throughout their life they fail at everything and feel unworthy to succeed. If someone speaks that you are dumb, a curse of dumbness follows you. Many say to their children, "I hate you, I wish you were never born!" A curse of rejection comes upon them because they believe the lie.

As I counsel with believers, I discover more and more of these sins and lies from the past that have haunted them for many years. The only way to freedom for them is to agree with God. They have to recognize that the enemy used people in the past to hurt them and to speak lies upon them in order to destroy them. They have to begin to see themselves as <u>God</u> sees them, and not as <u>they</u> think they are. This way of thinking and faith brings freedom.

> **Psalm 109:2–3** *For they have opened the wicked and deceitful mouth against me; they have spoken against me with a lying tongue. They have also surrounded me with words of hatred, and fought against me without cause.*

> **Psalm 109:17–20** *He also loved cursing, so it came to him; and he did not delight in blessing, so it was far from him. But he clothed himself with cursing as with his garment, and it entered into his body like water and like oil into his bones. Let it be to him as a garment with which he covers himself, and for a belt with which he constantly girds himself. Let this be the reward of my accusers from*

the Lord, and of those who speak evil against my soul.

None of these weapons and lies can have any power over the believer in Christ. This is your heritage—unless you choose to believe the lies.

> **Isaiah 54:17** *"No weapon that is formed against you will prosper; and every tongue that accuses you in judgment you will condemn. This is the heritage of the servants of the Lord, and their vindication is from Me," declares the Lord.*

Curses Evoked By Objects in Your Possession

An object in and of itself has no power of its own. Yet an object with an attached false belief does carry a curse. When an object is created for the purpose of worshipping or glorifying a false god or belief, demon power is denoted to it.

These objects may be in the form of jewelry, games, children's toys, religious items, statues, crafted items, carved items, books, movies, and music to name a few. Today's society is infatuated with the occult and new age thinking. Many believers have in their homes some of these things. The believer would have to be very ignorant to even allow such things to be a part of their life. Being unaware of the curses and demonic power present in their homes, many families fight, witness strange events, experience poverty, or deal with many other factors of defeat in their lives.

When I counsel with believers, I always address the issue of ungodly objects in their possession. I find believers with Ouija boards, Indian craft items such as dream catchers, horoscope items, new age items, etc. Sadly, these things are prominent in the homes of believers! God warns us against having such things, as it would ensnare the believer and his family. God always had the Jewish people destroy the false gods, so they would not fall into the sins and deceptions and be defeated by them.

> **Numbers 33:51–52** *Speak to the sons of Israel and say to*

them, "When you cross over the Jordan into the land of Canaan, then you shall drive out all the inhabitants of the land from before you, and <u>destroy</u> all their figured stones, and <u>destroy</u> all their molten images and <u>demolish</u> all their high places;

Psalm 106:35–43 *But they mingled with the nations and learned their practices, and served their idols, which became a snare to them. They even sacrificed their sons and their daughters <u>to the demons</u>, and shed innocent blood, the blood of their sons and their daughters, whom they sacrificed to the idols of Canaan; and the land was polluted with the blood. Thus they became unclean in their practices, and played the harlot in their deeds. Therefore the anger of the LORD was kindled against His people and He abhorred His inheritance. Then He gave them into the hand of the nations, and those who hated them ruled over them. Their enemies also oppressed them, and they were subdued under their power. Many times He would deliver them; they, however, were rebellious in their counsel, and so sank down in their iniquity.*

Even in the New Testament God desires the occult objects to be destroyed.

Acts 19:19 *And many of those who practiced magic brought their **books** together and began burning them in the sight of everyone; and they counted up the price of them and found it fifty thousand pieces of silver.* (In today's value, a few million dollars)

Ephesians 5:7–8,11 *Therefore <u>do not be partakers with them</u>; for you were formerly darkness, but now you are Light in the Lord; walk as children of Light*

<u>Do not participate in the unfruitful deeds of darkness</u>, but instead even expose them;

God wants these things that are an abomination destroyed!

Some Things to Look for and Destroy in Your Home:

Anything and everything...
- that is of the Indian religion, including the popular "dream catcher." Many do not realize that the Indian religion is a form of witchcraft
- that can be considered an idol, such as Mexican sun gods
- that is an occult object, such as Ouija boards
- attributed to false doctrines and/or witchcraft, such as Buddhas, hand-carved objects from Africa, the Caribbean islands, and the Orient

Anything connected with...
- astrology, horoscopes, fortune-telling
- all New Age beliefs
- books or objects associated with witchcraft
- good luck charms
- cults and false religions (Metaphysics, Christian Science, Jehovah's Witnesses, Catholicism, Masonic Lodge, etc...)
- heavy metal rock and rap records and tapes, CDs, and movie tapes

Some Things to Look for and Destroy From Your Children's Lives:

- Poke'Mon, Digimon, and Cardcaptors
- Harry Potter, Dungeons & Dragons
- Smurfs, Unicorns, Troll Dolls, and Sailor Moon
- Magic Eight Ball
- Power Rangers, Ninja Turtles, any and all things that attribute powers other than to Christ *alone*

Note: These lists contain only a very few items out of literally thousands!

Conclusion:

Curses can bring defeat, failure, shame, sickness, poverty, and even physical death to those who *reject* Christ. Those who do not accept this truth become more angry, self-righteous and defeated. They go deeper into bondage and darkness. As for the believer, curses are nothing but a lie that they choose to believe.

For the unbeliever, the Bible reveals that repentance to God is the approach for dealing with curses. For the believer, repentance to God for believing the lie and not submitting to truth is what is needed for victory. The believer needs to address both the personal sins and generational sins that they allowed into their life. Satan and his demons love to use these sins to cause grief and molestation in the believer's life.

I encourage you to seek God in this matter and allow him to disclose to you any sin patterns or lies that may be hindering you.

Curses?

132

Chapter 12

♦

Sickness and Mental Health

"Wow-I can't believe how much better I feel! I feel like a whole different person...it's so AWESOME. I was telling my husband last night about how you prayed for me and how God delivered me from a lot of stuff, and he said that he wouldn't mind talking to you some time."

Sickness and Mental Health

irst, let me start out by saying that <u>not all sickness is demonic</u>. Some sickness is due to the sin curse upon the earth. However, I will say that more than likely, many sicknesses and diseases are due to a demonic affliction. Many Scriptures show sickness and demons tied together during a person's healing.

There are also Scriptures that show just a sickness (with no associated demon) being cured. For instance, a fever had come upon Peter's mother-in-law and Jesus just commanded the fever to go, with no reference to a demon (Luke 4:39). Jesus healed many with no demonic connections. But we will be studying demonic sickness below as a part of the spiritual warfare teaching.

The Book of Job shows that Satan can bring forth sickness:

> **Job 2:7** *So Satan went out from the presence of the LORD and afflicted Job with painful sores from the soles of his feet to the top of his head* (NIV).

Satan sends his demons to induce sickness and afflict the bodies of believers. This is not the only way he afflicts them, but it is certainly one way he does. This confounds the minds of many modern-day believers. They cannot grasp this truth. It is contrary to everything they believe and have been wrongly taught.

"Spirits Of Infirmity"

When the Bible says a "Spirit of Infirmity," we read it and just pass over it with not much thought about it. What are these spirits? What do they do? What relationship do they have to a person being sick or having a disease? "Spirits of infirmity" are a specific group of demons whose sole purpose is to inflict sickness, disease, and pain on the body.

In Luke 13:11–16, Jesus healed a woman afflicted (for 18 years) with a bent-over back. He said that she had been bound by Satan. He also said that she had a "Spirit":

> *And there was a woman who for eighteen years had had a sickness caused by a spirit; and she was bent double, and could not straighten up at all. When Jesus saw her, He*

called her over and said to her, "Woman, you are freed from your sickness." And He laid His hands on her; and immediately she was made erect again and began glorifying God. But the synagogue official, indignant because Jesus had healed on the Sabbath, began saying to the crowd in response, "There are six days in which work should be done; so come during them and get healed, and not on the Sabbath day." But the Lord answered him and said, "You hypocrites, does not each of you on the Sabbath untie his ox or his donkey from the stall and lead him away to water him? And this woman, a daughter of Abraham as she is, whom Satan has bound for eighteen long years, should she not have been released from this bond on the Sabbath day?"

Something For You to Think About

If this woman were living in today's society, she would have gone to the doctor or clinic in her town to get a diagnosis or a medicine. Most likely they would have diagnosed her with arthritis in her back, and/or curvature of the spine, slipped discs, etc. She would be given pills and all kinds of treatments, but to no avail. She would not be cured, but only find some temporary relief. Nobody would have diagnosed her with having a spirit of infirmity. No one tried to stop Jesus by saying, "Hey, let's run tests and prescribe herbs or medicine to help ease the pain." Makes you wonder, doesn't it?

The Healing of a Boy with a Demon

Matthew 17:15–18 *"Lord, have mercy on my son, for he is a lunatic and is very ill; for he often falls into the fire and often into the water. I brought him to Your disciples, and they could not cure him." And Jesus answered and said, "You unbelieving and perverted generation, how long shall I be with you? How long shall I put up with you? Bring him here to Me." And Jesus rebuked him, and the demon*

136

came out of him, and the boy was cured at once.

Sounds like the boy above would have been diagnosed as having epileptic fits or brain disorders, and possibly be put in a mental hospital. I wonder how many people in those institutions just have demons? Again, this boy today would have been brought to a psychiatrist and/or treated for mental problems with a pill. The diagnosis would be that he has a chemical imbalance or is bi-polar. Yet he would live with this demon and never be cured unless someone was to do what Jesus had done!

Spirits of Infirmity and Sickness in Scripture

Many Scriptures show that numerous sicknesses are tied together with demons; these below are but a few:

> **Matthew 9:32–33** *As they were going out, a **mute**, demon-possessed man was brought to Him. After the demon was cast out, the mute man spoke; and the crowds were amazed, and were saying, "Nothing like this has ever been seen in Israel."*

> **Matthew 12:22** *Then a demon-possessed man who was **blind** and **mute** was brought to Jesus, and He healed him, so that the mute man spoke and saw.*

> **Mark 9:25** *When Jesus saw that a crowd was rapidly gathering, He rebuked the **unclean spirit**, saying to it, "You **deaf and mute spirit**, I command you, come out of him and do not enter him again."*

> **Luke 6:18** *who had come to hear Him and to be healed of their **diseases**; and those who were troubled with **unclean spirits** were being cured.*

> **Luke 7:21** *At that very time He cured many people of **diseases and afflictions and evil spirits**; and He gave sight to many who were blind.*

Luke 8:2 *and also some women who had been healed of* ***evil spirits and sicknesses****: Mary who was called Magdalene, from whom seven demons had gone out,*

I counsel with so many people who are demonized. Many have a sickness that never goes away. It could be mental or physical, and yet it binds them. Many are depressed and go to doctors to get pills with no cure. The pills help mask the symptoms, but they are still depressed. They try to cure a spiritual problem with a magic pill. This is the reasonable outcome, since many are deceived into thinking that demons are not real—or were only present in Biblical times.

Let me share a testimony with you:

I recently counseled a lady in her 40's. She was extremely depressed and suicidal. She had been this way since childhood. For all these years, she had gone to psychologists and medical doctors, who prescribed her all kinds of pills and anti-depressants. To no avail: she was still depressed, with suicidal thoughts and a marriage and family about to split up. A mutual friend recommended that she get spiritual warfare counseling with me. We met, and inside of 3 hours of counsel and deliverance, she was completely set free!

She chose of her own accord to throw out all medications, quit all doctors, and is now living free of depression and suicide. She now serves God and the whole family has come to Jesus! She got in that condition from demons of unforgiveness who entered her by things done to her in her childhood.

Demons of infirmity and mental torment are real...just like the Bible says. If the demons had not been cast out of the lady in the above story, she would still be depressed today and would have possibly lost her family as well; worse yet, committed suicide. I truly believe that most, if not all, mental patients are demonized, and all they need is knowledge of the Word of God and Biblical deliverance.

Always seek God on the matter at the same time you seek out medical attention. It could just be a demon! Now I also know that God sometimes uses doctors to carry out his healings, but I suggest you seek His will *first*.

Multiple Personality Disorder

Multiple Personality Disorder (or MPD for short) is a subject of great controversy. In all my years of doing deliverance, I have run into those who are not only demonized, but also have multiple personalities besides. I would guess around 5% of the demonized Christians I work with have this problem. Also, this seems to affect more women than men; most likely because women are usually abused or molested more often than men, and women have a general tendency to be more emotionally unstable.

There is no denying the fact that MPD does exist. It is a very real part of the traumatized mind. You may be asking, "How does one acquire MPD?" Well to begin with, when a person (usually at a very young age) experiences deep pain, trauma, or emotional hurt and/or abuse, the mind is split into a disassociation of that time period.

Example: If a little girl, at 5 years of age, is molested by her dad or someone in a trusting position, the pain and trauma of that event is encapsulated in the mind as a way of dealing with it. Later, that same woman (maybe at the age of 35 or so) may sometimes act or speak like a 5-year old child. She might have a deep hatred or resentment towards all men and not know why. This happens only at particular times—especially when memories are recalled strongly. And when trying to recall that time or event in counseling, she may respond as a crying 5-year old child or a very angry lady.

There are those who preach false doctrines, such as the idea that multiple personalities are gifts from God. These are nothing but pure lies. Man's wisdom and thinking is far from God's and is futile. The fact remains that multiple personalities are indeed strongholds of Satan and not of God! Those with MPD are always in a state of confusion and fear. God is not the author of confusion or fear, but Satan is. MPD's are usually depressed, and live in a state of turmoil. None of these can be attributed to God.

The world's way of dealing with MPD may appear to work; yet it fails for it is not Biblical. The doctors even perpetuate the idea to the MPD victim that the personalities are real people sharing the one body. How ridiculous! God says we are to be of sound mind consisting of hope, joy, peace, and faith!

> **2 Timothy 1:7** *For God did not give us a spirit of timidity, but a spirit of power, of love and of self-discipline.* (NIV)

> **Romans 8:15** *For you have not received a spirit of slavery leading to fear again, but you have received a spirit of adoption as sons by which we cry out, "Abba! Father!"* (NIV)

> **Romans 15:13** *Now may the God of hope fill you with all joy and peace in believing, so that you will abound in hope by the power of the Holy Spirit.*

There are those who also preach that alter personalities are actually demon spirits. This also is wrong. Demons can be commanded—and a believer has authority over them in Christ—but not alters. Alters are a part of the person, and they do not respond as a demon spirit *must*. Believers do not have authority over fellow man. Many preachers and counselors try to mix spiritual things with human psychology. They are convinced that one must have lengthy conversations with each personality, trying to convince it of its wrong. However, teaching the Word of God to the *whole* person releases them from the lies and points of pain.

We are to be people of faith. I have worked with many MPD's, and guess what? When the demons are cast out, and the person is shown truth, the alter personalities are gone also. Why? Because the demons hide behind the points of pain and trauma in that person's mind, to control and dominate them in the fear and terror of the past. This is more evidence that MPD's are not a gift from God, but a stronghold of the enemy.

The truth will set you free! (John 8:31-32) Knowledge of God's Word and written promises is what brings freedom to the mind. The Bible tells us to renew and transform our mind and thinking…to think on things above and to take captive every thought to make it obedient to Christ! The enemy comes to steal, kill and destroy. He uses lies and accusations of the past as a way of taking you captive.

If you want freedom from MPD for yourself or someone you love, repentance to God and agreeing with God is a must. But most of all, you must forgive EVERYONE who has ever hurt you in the past. This takes the legal rights away from the demons operating the MPD stronghold. God will deliver you when you forgive others. When you do this He will heal you and deliver you from demons, as well as a confused mind. You can and will be made whole…as you were created to be!

Chapter 13

◆

Deliverance and Counseling
(and Demon Groupings)

"All I want to be able to do is to be free and stop the self-harming. I am tired of lying about the scars. I am tired of putting a mask on for people. I just want to be real. I really love the Lord..."

very believer can cast out demons (Mark 16:17).
Unfortunately, there are not many believers that even have a clue about the reality of demonization. Believers can have many demons. Proper deliverance and counsel takes time and knowledge. <u>One must be led by the Holy Spirit and abide in Christ</u>.

Here we will be learning some basic steps in leading yourself or another believer out of captivity and bondage. Whether you suspect that you yourself or someone else has demons, the same principles apply in either case. However, sometimes a believer cannot help himself because of interfering demonic activity. If this were the case, that believer would need to seek out another believer to take them through the steps. The following is an outline that I myself use and also teach to my ministry team. *All deliverances must be led by the Holy Spirit...in every case.*

Before going through the steps of deliverance, I would like to discuss what you will need as a deliverance counselor. The ministering person or persons need support. By this, I mean others who are in prayer for the ministering person or persons. Also, I highly recommend that the ministering person have at least one other person as an assistant during deliverance and counseling times. This is most important: that a man and a woman never be alone. This would give opportunity for the flesh to hinder God, as well as the demons would seek to discredit the ministering person. An assistant would also be available if there are strong demonic manifestations. The assistant can also be beneficial for prayer and the taking of notes.

The other things needed are: the Bible, of course, and an understanding of God's Word. Always counsel someone with God's Word and not just your opinion. Remember, truth is what sets one free. Be sure to have plenty of paper and a pen for notes. It is vital that as you counsel the victim you write down the specifics of the sins and struggles they have. These notes will be of great value later so you can recall each sin, area of disobedience, or legal grounds the demons have. The notes will also reveal the generational sin patterns as well. (See Appendix "C" at end of manual.)

Be sure to have light refreshments available for comfort, as well as being sure there are no items in the room that could hurt someone physically. The drinks should be served in plastic, not glass. Be sure all sharp objects are removed for everyone's safety. This is a good precaution in case of demonic manifestation. The temperature should be comfortable for all involved. Turn off phones and beepers. There is nothing worse than being interrupted by these during deliverance. Low-playing praise music would be fine; however, if it becomes a hindrance, then turn it off.

Now, with these issues addressed, let's look at the steps to freedom.

The ABC's of Counseling

Prior to these steps the person who is doing the counseling, and being the willing vessel for Jesus Christ the Lord to work through, should examine himself for sin and disobedience, or lack of submitting to the Lord. In order for someone to operate in the authority of Christ, he himself must be in submission to that authority.

A) Always begin with prayer and seek God's guidance through the Holy Spirit for everyone involved in the deliverance. This step may even take place days or weeks in advance. Be sure to take authority over the demonic realm to keep them from hindering you while ministering to their victim.

B) Begin by assuring the victim, which allows them to trust you. You must also be sure to commit yourself to complete confidentiality for everyone involved. Make the victim comfortable, both emotionally as well as physically.

C) The session should then begin by giving the demonized person the opportunity to discuss his or her problems and background. This will allow you to get to know the victim and understand how to properly minister to them. Be sure at this time to take good notes. You may want to use the "Counseling Question Guide" included with this manual. (See Appendix "C" at end of Manual)

D) Ask questions as the victim divulges information. Sometimes, you must get them to go deeper and explain in more detail. Remember: your goal here is to disclose every possible open door for demonic activity. Remind the victim that if they want complete freedom they need to cooperate fully. If there are 10 things that need to be confessed they cannot give you 9. This will leave a door open for demons to come back after you cast them out.

E) Discuss the sins of the ancestors. Ask what sin or sins (including addictions, habits, and/or the occult) do they have that are same as one or both parents and/or grandparents. This is vital, since most demons are passed down this way from the iniquities of the forefathers.

F) Ask about any unforgiveness the victim has toward anyone—including themselves. I have found in 99.9 percent of the cases I work with, there is always unforgiveness. This is a common demonic doorway. Unforgiveness starts from being hurt. It then turns to bitterness, then anger, then hatred, and finally, to rage (see Chapter 2).

G) Once all is disclosed and written down, the next step is to apply the Word of God to each situation. Bring the person to an understanding of why each sin is wrong. Try to have them understand what God says in all things. Your goal here is to get the victim to see it God's way, and not their own. The victim must be brought to a place of being willing to turn to God; to be willing to repent, which means to change one's mind; to agree with God.

H) Having brought the victim to understanding, begin to discuss the next steps with them as listed in the next section of this chapter. The victim must be willing. If victim is willing and in agreement, then move on and apply these steps. If not, then deliverance stops here until they are ready. You cannot force someone to be free. The victim must desire it.

The 5 Steps to Freedom

The first two steps outlined here are in agreement with:

James 4:7 *Submit therefore to God. Resist the devil and he will flee from you.*

1) The victim will need to confess—out loud—each one of the sins they disclosed. (The ministering person may lead them in this, and also all other steps). The confession returns them to fellowship with God. Confession means "to say the same thing as God," or "to agree with God." The victim must choose to submit to God.

> Example: "Lord Jesus Christ, I confess to you that I have had unforgiveness toward my parents, and I choose at this time to forgive them from my heart. I also have been allowing fear and doubt to be a part of my life and I give those to you now as well. Deliver me, Lord, and restore fellowship unto me for your glory."

2) Lead the victim in verbally declaring and renouncing each and every sin and act of disobedience, and the works of the enemy. This is to proclaim before the demonic world his or her desire to break bonds with them and reclaim his or her authority. This is "resisting the enemy" as you submit to God.

> Example: "I renounce and reject all demons and your demonic lies. I renounce the spirits and lies of unforgiveness, fear, and doubt. I have chosen to submit to God in these areas and you have no more place or authority in my life as it is written in the name of Jesus Christ the Lord!"

3) You are now ready to <u>command </u>the demons to come out of the victim. Out loud, speak in authority to the demonic realm. "In

the name of the Lord Jesus Christ, and the fullness of Christ that dwells in me, Colossians 2:10, all demons in __*Victim's Name*__, you no longer have any authority in these areas. You are commanded to come out now! And return no more, in Jesus' name!"

At this point the victim *may* cough, hack, sneeze, vomit, or uncontrollably yawn. These are some signs of demons leaving the body. You should then notice a sense of peace come upon the freed victim. However, do not always look for an outward sign. Rely instead on the assurance of your faith, and on the discernment of the Holy Spirit.

4) Allow the freed victim to ponder the experience and to rest a minute or so. When ready, proceed to have the freed victim begin to thank and praise God for his or her deliverance.

5) The freed person must now be counseled and discipled in God's Word. <u>This step needs to be done as soon as possible</u>! I usually take the person through a small Bible study on renewing the mind. Then I place them with someone on my deliverance team to mentor and disciple them on a long-term basis. They are taught the things in this War Manual and taken through a deep Biblical study about who they are in Christ. They are taught how to live in victory and abide in God, how to forgive all the time, and how to walk in a manner worthy of their calling. Remember, the freed person needs truth and needs to love Jesus more. They must be filled with the things of God. If they stay empty, the demons can come back according to the following Scripture verse:

> **Mathew 12:43–45** *Now when the unclean spirit goes out of a man, it passes through waterless places seeking rest, and does not find it. Then it says, "I will return to my house from which I came; and when it comes, it finds it unoccupied, swept, and put in order. Then it goes and takes along with it seven other spirits more wicked than itself, and they go in and live there; and the last state of that man becomes worse than the first. That is the way it will also be with this evil generation."*

Common Demon Groupings Found in a Demonized Believer

Demon families, or groupings, are demons that are usually found together. For example, Rejection might be the chief demon or doorway that was the initial cause of demonization to come into the person's life. Once that stronghold was established, it may have opened the door for Bitterness and Rebellion to enter. You will discover these as you are counseling. The demon's name and/or function is the fruit it manifests in the victim.

In other words, if the victim is enslaved to being rejected, having hatred, and being deceived, then they have those demons in them. In step 3 of the previous section of this chapter, you may command the demons to come out by name according to the scenario just given. You may say, "Demons of Rejection, Hate, and Deception, come out of __Victim's Name__ now in Jesus' name!"

Below are only 10 of the most common demon groupings that I run into when counseling people. These are not written in stone. They just seem to be common when dealing with a demonized person. The combinations are unlimited. These are meant only as examples. As you minister, you will also discover these...as well as many others.

1) Rejection...Bitterness...Unforgiveness...Unworthiness
2) Hatred...Murder...Suicide
3) Anger...Rage...Abuse
4) Witchcraft...Control...Rebellion
5) Violence...Temper...Rage
6) Depression...Unforgiveness...Fear
7) Self-Rejection...Un-worthiness...Guilt
8) Self-Will...Rebellion...Stubbornness
9) Strife...Jealousy...Envy
10) Pride...Perfection...Criticism

Congratulations!

You are now discipled in the truth of correct spiritual warfare. It is time to help yourself, or others, to live a life of victory and assurance. The purpose statement for my ministry is:

> *"To free God's people that are held captive by the Devil, and to equip the people of God to do battle for the glory of God."*

So now I say to you, a soldier in the Lord's army, you are equipped through the study of God's Word in this manual. Now it is time to deliver God's people from their strongholds, and to restore them to their victory in Jesus.

Chapter 14

◆

Author's Closing Comments

"Even though I knew I had Christ in my heart, went to church, read my Bible, and prayed, I had picked up habits that were keeping me in bondage for over 20 years. When I first contacted Bill I was addicted to smoking and sleeping pills. I never understood exactly what I was doing to myself, others, or God until after speaking with Bill. I then knew this addiction to smoking and sleeping pills had to end. I had been smoking for over 20 years and on the pills for 10 years. He began to counsel and pray with me about my addictions. He stood in agreement with me to be delivered from them.

Finally, after many long years, I am completely delivered from both my addiction to pills and smoking.

I encourage all of you who know you have Christ—and yet are in some kind of bondage—to seek truth. I learned so much from Bill, and I can't tell you how relieved I am to have come to Bill and ask for help. My life is finally in order, and I am walking closer to God. I am more knowledgeable about demon influences and how to take authority over it.

He is able to recognize demon activity, influence, or bondage. He does speak the truth since everything is Scriptural. He is a man of honor and integrity. Praise God for people like Bill Niland, who dedicate themselves in a ministry for the purpose of glorifying God and seeing God's people set free from bondage. I know without a shadow of a doubt that the man has been called into this ministry. God is behind all that he does. He is equipped to handle any and all situations, no matter what the bondage or spiritual warfare may be. Thanks, Bill, for the guidance, prayers, support, and your stand to uphold truth to me no matter what."

ow that you have made it to the end of the manual, I ask you, "What is next?" It would be easy to set this War Manual on the shelf and move on. However, that was not my intent in writing it. My desire is that this material would motivate you to get up and do something...to practically apply this truth to your own life, as well as to others in the Body of Christ.

As you reflect on the truth in this manual, seek God on how to effectively apply it. Realize that everyone needs to be involved in spiritual warfare on the corporate level, as well as on a personal level—especially the fathers of families. God has placed the man as head of the household and spiritual leader over his family. Fathers and/or parents should be aware of the traps in each family that cause strife and division. Parents need to take the God-given authority they have and use it over each situation and the schemes of the enemy. The enemy steals from people and families everyday. Having been equipped with truth, now you can understand how to fight back.

The Body of Christ as a whole is suffering needlessly in this cosmic war. I ask that you consider teaching this and showing more of God's people the truth. God has shown me that his people are destroyed for a lack of this knowledge. Believers no longer have to live lives in defeat. This teaching is not new; no, it's always been part of our calling in Christ. Unfortunately, today's churches and leaders in an industrialized, modernized, self-fulfilling nation have been deceived. Most of what is taught in today's churches—which is widely considered Biblically correct—is what I call a "Fluffy Gospel."

Today's culture has infiltrated the churches. For example, medical marvels have replaced trusting in God's provisions and words. There is no pill to treat demons! No one even dares to consider the possibility that a person's problem might be a demon. Just give them a pill, and allow them to live with it or manage it. Many preachers are teaching nothing but "Let's get along and love everybody of all religions and backgrounds. Don't worry about what God says; that was all back in old Bible days."

Most believers are not being discipled in the truth of all of God's word. Many get saved and are left alone to fend for themselves. They are quickly devoured by the enemy's lies. Believers who have known the Lord for 20 years or more are still feeling defeated and hopeless. They run to the pastors and say, "Will I ever have victory?" The preachers answer is to study more, do devotionals more, pray more, get involved more, or some fluffy answer. Nothing but pure legalism and guilt trips.

God's people have plenty of basic knowledge or spiritual milk. However, many pastors and preachers only "drink" milk themselves. How can you teach what you do not know or understand yourself? God's people need to be fully equipped in all areas of truth. One of these areas is spiritual warfare.

Study this War Manual over and over again. Begin to apply it as you seek God. Watch what happens! Your Christian walk will come to life. You will live with a new attitude and state of assurance. You will know and taste victory. You can take back all the enemy has stolen from you or your family.

God will go with you, but <u>you</u> must get up and go as King David did in 1 Samuel chapter 30. The Lord has given all of His children the tools and promises to have victory. Believers have armor and weapons for using in faith. God does not give them to you so you can keep them in some spiritual closet! *He* is the power and might behind them; yet as believers, we are still required to have faith to use them. We are required to show action. After all, faith without works is dead!

My Prayer for You

My Lord and Savior Jesus Christ, I humbly come before you to seek your face and will. Lord, I ask and pray that the ones who read and study this manual will have their eyes opened to the truth. Lord, it is so you are glorified, and that your Kingdom and Power will be preached throughout all lands.

Lord, give each person studying this manual the strength to stand not only against the enemy, but even against those professing believers who are captured by the enemy, who are against this truth from being known. Lord, you had said that we are blessed when persecuted for your name's sake. May each individual be blessed.

Lord, as these truths are applied in their lives, deliver them from the evil ones. Guide and show each person the hidden things.

Expose the enemy in all areas in and around their life. Lord, as you have promised, the truth will set them free!
   In Jesus' name, Amen.

Peace and strength be unto you,

Bill Nула

Appendix A

♦

Your Identity in Christ

This comprehensive list of Scriptures shows the believer, through God's Word, his identity in Christ. These identities are all automatic at the moment of salvation. They are the titles God gives the believer, and how God views the believer. This is also the result of the new creation, which the believer must now see himself as. Part of understanding how to walk in victory is accepting these characteristics that you, as a believer, possess.

The Believer's Relationship with God:

Reconciled:
2 Corinthians 5:18

> *Now all these things are from God, who <u>reconciled</u> us to Himself through Christ and gave us the ministry of reconciliation,*

Child of God:
1 John 3:1–2

> *See how great a love the Father has bestowed on us, that we would be called <u>children</u> of God; and such we are. For this reason the world does not know us, because it did not know Him. Beloved, now we are <u>children</u> of God, and it has not appeared as yet what we will be. We know that when He appears, we will be like Him, because we will see Him just as He is.*

Saints:
1 Corinthians 1:2

> *To the church of God which is at Corinth, to those who have been sanctified in Christ Jesus, <u>saints</u> by calling, with all who in every place call on the name of our Lord Jesus Christ, their Lord and ours.*

Christ's friend:

John 15:15

> *No longer do I call you slaves, for the slave does not know what his master is doing; but I have called you friends, for all things that I have heard from My Father I have made known to you.*

Citizen of God's Kingdom:

Ephesians 2:19

> *So then you are no longer strangers and aliens, but you are fellow citizens with the saints, and are of God's household,*

Born of God:

1 John 4:7

> *Beloved, let us love one another, for love is from God; and everyone who loves is born of God and knows God.*

Near to Christ:

Ephesians 2:13

> *But now in Christ Jesus you who formerly were far off have been brought near by the blood of Christ.*

Adopted by God:

Romans 8:15

> *For you have not received a spirit of slavery leading to fear again, but you have received a spirit of adoption as sons by which we cry out, Abba! Father!*

Likeness of God's Righteousness and Holiness:

Ephesians 4:24

> *and put on the new self, which in the likeness of God has been created in righteousness and holiness of the truth.*

Direct access to God:
Ephesians 2:18
> *for through Him we both have our <u>access</u> in one Spirit to the Father.*

The Believer's Inheritance

Heir of God:
Romans 8:17
> *and if children, <u>heirs</u> also, <u>heirs</u> of God and fellow <u>heirs</u> with Christ, if indeed we suffer with Him so that we may also be glorified with Him.*

Delivered from Satan's kingdom:
Colossians 1:13
> *For He <u>rescued us from the domain of darkness</u>, and transferred us to the kingdom of His beloved Son,*

Hidden in Christ:
Colossians 3:3
> *For you have died and your life is <u>hidden</u> with Christ in God.*

Spiritual blessings:
Ephesians 1:3
> *Blessed be the God and Father of our Lord Jesus Christ, who has blessed us with every <u>spiritual blessing</u> in the heavenly places in Christ,*

Chosen of God:
Colossians 3:12
> *So, as those who have been <u>chosen of God</u>, holy and beloved, put on a heart of compassion, kindness, humility, gentleness and patience;*

Child of Light:
1 Thessalonians 5:5
> *for you are all <u>sons of light</u> and sons of day. We are not of night nor of darkness;*

Partaker of Christ:
Hebrews 3:14
> *For we have become <u>partakers of Christ</u>, if we hold fast the beginning of our assurance firm until the end,*

Living Stones:
1 Peter 2:5
> *you also, as <u>living stones</u>, are being built up as a spiritual house for a holy priesthood, to offer up spiritual sacrifices acceptable to God through Jesus Christ.*

Citizen of Heaven:
Philippians 3:20
> *But our <u>citizenship</u> is in heaven. And we eagerly await a Savior from there, the Lord Jesus Christ,*

The Believer's Transformation

Chosen Race, Royal Priesthood, A Holy Nation, A People for God:
1 Peter 2:9
> *But you are a <u>chosen race</u>, a <u>royal priesthood</u>, a <u>holy nation</u>, <u>a people for God's</u> own possession, so that you may proclaim the excellencies of Him who has called you out of darkness into His marvelous light;*

Redeemed and forgiven:
Ephesians 1:6–8
> *In Him we have <u>redemption</u> through His blood, the <u>forgiveness</u> of our trespasses, according to the riches of His*

grace which He lavished on us. In all wisdom and insight.

Aliens and strangers:
1 Peter 2:11

> *Beloved, I urge you as <u>aliens</u> and <u>strangers</u> to abstain from fleshly lusts which wage war against the soul.*

Justified:
Romans 5:1

> *Therefore, having been <u>justified</u> by faith, we have peace with God through our Lord Jesus Christ,*

Enemy of Satan:
1 Peter 5:8

> *Be of sober spirit, be on the alert. Your <u>adversary</u>, the devil, prowls around like a roaring lion, seeking someone to devour.*

Eternal life:
John 5:24

> *Truly, truly, I say to you, he who hears My word, and believes Him who sent Me, has <u>eternal life</u>, and does not come into judgment, but has passed out of death into life.*

Anointed:
1 John 2:27

> *As for you, the <u>anointing</u> you received from him remains in you, and you do not need anyone to teach you. But as his <u>anointing</u> teaches you about all things and as that <u>anointing</u> is real, not counterfeit—just as it has taught you, remain in him.*

The Believer's Calling

Free from condemnation:
Romans 8:1
> *Therefore there is now <u>no condemnation</u> for those who are in Christ Jesus.*

Salt of the earth:
Matthew 5:13
> *You are the <u>salt of the earth</u>; but if the salt has become tasteless, how can it be made salty again? It is no longer good for anything, except to be thrown out and trampled under foot by men.*

Light of the world:
Matthew 5:14
> *You are the <u>light of the world</u>. A city set on a hill cannot be hidden;*

Have the mind of Christ:
1 Corinthians 2:16
> *For who has known the mind of the Lord, that he will instruct Him? But <u>we have the mind of Christ</u>.*

Chosen, and appointed to bear fruit:
John 15:16
> *You did not choose Me but I <u>chose you</u>, and <u>appointed</u> you that you would go and <u>bear fruit</u>, and that your fruit would remain, so that whatever you ask of the Father in My name He may give to you.*

Crucified with Christ:
Galatians 2:20
> *I have been <u>crucified with Christ</u>; and it is no longer I who*

live, but Christ lives in me; and the life which I now live in the flesh I live by faith in the Son of God, who loved me and gave Himself up for me.

<u>Called to do the works of Christ:</u>
John 14:12

> *Truly, truly, I say to you, he who believes in Me, the works that I do, <u>he will do also</u>; and greater works than these he will do; because I go to the Father.*

<u>New Creation:</u>
2 Corinthians 5:17

> *Therefore if anyone is in Christ, he is a <u>new creature</u>; the old things passed away; behold, new things have come.*

<u>Alive in Christ</u>
Ephesians 2:5

> *even when we were dead in our transgressions, made us <u>alive together with Christ</u> (by grace you have been saved),*

<u>Given spiritual authority:</u>
Luke 10:19

> *Behold, <u>I have given you authority</u> to tread on serpents and scorpions, and over all the power of the enemy, and nothing will injure you.*

<u>God's workmanship:</u>
Ephesians 2:10

> *For we are <u>His workmanship</u>, created in Christ Jesus for good works, which God prepared beforehand so that we would walk in them.*

Complete in Christ:
Colossians 2:10

> *and in Him you have been made complete, and He is the head over all rule and authority;*

Ministers of the New Covenant
2 Corinthians 3:6

> *who also made us adequate as servants of a new covenant, not of the letter but of the Spirit; for the letter kills, but the Spirit gives life.*

Ministers of reconciliation:
2 Corinthians 5:18

> *Now all these things are from God, who reconciled us to Himself through Christ and gave us the ministry of reconciliation,*

Equipped for good works:
2 Timothy 3:17

> *so that the man of God may be thoroughly equipped for every good work.*

The Believer's Position in Christ

Peace of Christ to rule:
Colossians 3:15

> *Let the peace of Christ rule in your hearts, to which indeed you were called in one body; and be thankful.*

Connected to the true vine:
John 15:5

> *I am the vine, you are the branches; he who abides in Me and I in him, he bears much fruit, for apart from Me you can do nothing.*

Partakers of a heavenly calling:
Hebrews 3:1
> *Therefore, holy brethren, partakers of a heavenly calling,*
> *consider Jesus, the Apostle and High Priest of our*
> *confession;*

Slave to righteousness:
Romans 6:18
> *and having been freed from sin, you became <u>slaves of</u>*
> *<u>righteousness</u>.*

Temple of God:
1 Corinthians 3:16
> *Do you not know that you are a <u>temple of God</u> and that the*
> *Spirit of God dwells in you?*

One Spirit with Christ:
1 Corinthians 6:17
> *But the one who joins himself to the Lord is <u>one spirit with</u>*
> *<u>Him.</u>*

Member of Christ's body:
1 Corinthians 12:27
> *Now you are Christ's body, and individually <u>members</u> of it.*

Ambassadors for Christ:
2 Corinthians 5:20
> *We are therefore Christ's <u>ambassadors</u>, as though God*
> *were making his appeal through us. We implore you on*
> *Christ's behalf: Be reconciled to God.*

Soldier:
2 Timothy 2:3–4
> *Endure hardship with us like a good <u>soldier</u> of Christ*

Jesus. No one serving as a <u>soldier</u> gets involved in civilian affairs—he wants to please his commanding officer.

<u>Overcomer:</u>
1 John 5:4

> *for everyone born of God <u>overcomes</u> the world. This is the victory that has overcome the world, even our faith.*

<u>Conqueror:</u>
Romans 8:37

> *No, in all these things we are more than <u>conquerors</u> through him who loved us.*

Appendix B

◆

Demons in Scripture

This is a compiled list of demons mentioned in the Bible. However, this list is not comprehensive. I chose only the ones that seemed to stand out the most. None of these Scriptures include any mention of Satan himself, as this was discussed at length in chapter 3. All Scripture verses are taken from the NASB version of the Bible. Scriptures from both the Old Testament and the New Testament are included. This is a great tool to use as a handy, quick reference.

Old Testament

Leviticus 17:7 *They shall no longer sacrifice their sacrifices to the <u>goat demons</u> with which they play the harlot. This shall be a permanent statute to them throughout their generations.*

Numbers 5:14 *if a <u>spirit of jealousy</u> comes over him and he is jealous of his wife when she has defiled herself, or if a spirit of jealousy comes over him and he is jealous of his wife when she has not defiled herself,*

Numbers 5:30 *or when a <u>spirit of jealousy</u> comes over a man and he is jealous of his wife, he shall then make the woman stand before the LORD, and the priest shall apply all this law to her.*

Deuteronomy 32:17 *They sacrificed to <u>demons</u> who were not God, to gods whom they have not known, new gods who came lately, whom your fathers did not dread.*

1 Kings 22:21–23 *Then <u>a spirit</u> came forward and stood before the LORD and said, "I will entice him." The LORD said to him, "How?" And he said, "I will go out and be a <u>deceiving spirit</u> in the mouth of all his prophets." Then He said, "You are to entice him and also prevail. Go and do so." Now therefore, behold, the LORD has put a <u>deceiving spirit</u> in the mouth of all these your prophets; and the LORD has proclaimed disaster against you.*

Psalm 106:37 *They even sacrificed their sons and their daughters to the <u>demons</u>,*

Isaiah 19:3 *Then the <u>spirit of the Egyptians</u> will be demoralized within them; and I will confound their strategy, so that they will resort to idols and ghosts of the dead and to mediums and spiritists.*

Zechariah 13:2 *"It will come about in that day," declares the LORD of hosts, "that I will cut off the names of the idols from the land, and they will no longer be remembered; and I will also remove the prophets and the <u>unclean spirit</u> from the land."*

New Testament

Matthew 4:24 *The news about Him spread throughout all Syria; and they brought to Him all who were ill, those suffering with various diseases and pains, <u>demoniacs</u>, epileptics, paralytics; and He healed them.*

Matthew 7:22 *Many will say to Me on that day, "Lord, Lord, did we not prophesy in Your name, and in Your name cast out <u>demons</u>, and in Your name perform many miracles?"*

Matthew 8:16 *When evening came, they brought to Him many who were <u>demon</u>-possessed; and He cast out the spirits with a word, and healed all who were ill.*

Matthew 8:28 *When He came to the other side into the country of the Gadarenes, two men who were <u>demon</u>-possessed met Him as they were coming out of the tombs. They were so extremely violent that no one could pass by that way.*

Matthew 8:31 *the <u>demons</u> began to entreat Him, saying, "If You are going to cast us out, send us into the herd of swine."*

Matthew 8:33 *The herdsmen ran away, and went to the city and* *reported everything, including what had happened to the* <u>*demoniacs.*</u>

Matthew 9:32 *As they were going out, a mute,* <u>*demon*</u>*-possessed man was brought to Him.*

Matthew 9:33 *After the* <u>*demon*</u> *was cast out, the mute man spoke; and the crowds were amazed, and were saying, "Nothing like this has ever been seen in Israel."*

Matthew 9:34 *But the Pharisees were saying, "He casts out the demons by the ruler of the* <u>*demons.*</u>*"*

Matthew 10:1 *Jesus summoned His twelve disciples and gave them authority over* <u>*unclean spirits*</u>*, to cast them out, and to heal every kind of disease and every kind of sickness.*

Matthew 10:8 *Heal the sick, raise the dead, cleanse the lepers, cast out* <u>*demons*</u>*. Freely you received, freely give.*

Matthew 11:18 *For John came neither eating nor drinking, and they say, "He has a* <u>*demon!*</u>*"*

Matthew 12:22 *Then a* <u>*demon*</u>*-possessed man who was blind and mute was brought to Jesus, and He healed him, so that the mute man spoke and saw.*

Matthew 12:24 *But when the Pharisees heard this, they said, "This man casts out demons only by Beelzebul the ruler of the* <u>*demons.*</u>*"*

Matthew 12:27 *If I by Beelzebul cast out* <u>*demons*</u>*, by whom do your sons cast them out? For this reason they will be your judges.*

Matthew 12:28 *But if I cast out* <u>*demons*</u> *by the Spirit of God, then the kingdom of God has come upon you.*

Matthew 12:43 *Now when the* <u>*unclean spirit*</u> *goes out of a man, it passes through waterless places seeking rest, and does not find it.*

Matthew 12:45 *Then it goes and takes along with it <u>seven other spirits</u> more wicked than itself, and they go in and live there; and the last state of that man becomes worse than the first. That is the way it will also be with this evil generation.*

Matthew 15:22 *And a Canaanite woman from that region came out and began to cry out, saying, "Have mercy on me, Lord, Son of David; my daughter is cruelly <u>demon</u>-possessed."*

Matthew 17:18 *And Jesus rebuked him, and the <u>demon</u> came out of him, and the boy was cured at once.*

Mark 1:23 *Just then there was a man in their synagogue with an <u>unclean spirit</u>; and he cried out,*

Mark 1:26 *Throwing him into convulsions, the <u>unclean spirit</u> cried out with a loud voice and came out of him.*

Mark 1:27 *They were all amazed, so that they debated among themselves, saying, "What is this? A new teaching with authority! He commands even the <u>unclean spirits,</u> and they obey Him."*

Mark 1:32 *When evening came, after the sun had set, they began bringing to Him all who were ill and those who were <u>demon</u>-possessed.*

Mark 1:34 *And He healed many who were ill with various diseases, and cast out many <u>demons</u>; and He was not permitting the demons to speak, because they knew who He was.*

Mark 1:39 *And He went into their synagogues throughout all Galilee, preaching and casting out the <u>demons.</u>*

Mark 3:11 *Whenever the <u>unclean spirits</u> saw Him, they would fall down before Him and shout, "You are the Son of God!"*

Mark 3:30 *because they were saying, "He has an <u>unclean spirit</u>."*

Mark 5:2 *When He got out of the boat, immediately a man from the tombs with an <u>unclean spirit</u> met Him,*

Mark 5:8 *For He had been saying to him, "Come out of the man, you <u>unclean spirit</u>!"*

Mark 5:13 *Jesus gave them permission. And coming out, the <u>unclean spirits</u> entered the swine; and the herd rushed down the steep bank into the sea, about two thousand of them; and they were drowned in the sea.*

Mark 5:15 *They came to Jesus and observed the man who had been <u>demon</u>-possessed sitting down, clothed and in his right mind, the very man who had had the "legion"; and they became frightened.*

Mark 5:16 *Those who had seen it described to them how it had happened to the <u>demon</u>-possessed man, and all about the swine.*

Mark 5:18 *As He was getting into the boat, the man who had been <u>demon</u>-possessed was imploring Him that he might accompany Him.*

Mark 6:7 *And He summoned the twelve and began to send them out in pairs, and gave them authority over the <u>unclean spirits</u>;*

Mark 7:25 *But after hearing of Him, a woman whose little daughter had an <u>unclean spirit</u> immediately came and fell at His feet.*

Mark 7:26 *Now the woman was a Gentile, of the Syrophoenician race. And she kept asking Him to cast the <u>demon</u> out of her daughter.*

Mark 7:30 *And going back to her home, she found the child lying on the bed, the <u>demon</u> having left.*

Mark 9:25 *When Jesus saw that a crowd was rapidly gathering, He rebuked the unclean spirit, saying to it, "<u>You deaf and mute</u>*

spirit, I command you, come out of him and do not enter him again."

Luke 4:33 *In the synagogue there was a man possessed by the <u>spirit of an unclean demon</u>, and he cried out with a loud voice,*

Luke 4:35 *But Jesus rebuked him, saying, "Be quiet and come out of him!" And when the <u>demon</u> had thrown him down in the midst of the people, he came out of him without doing him any harm.*

Luke 4:36 *And amazement came upon them all, and they began talking with one another saying, "What is this message? For with authority and power He commands the <u>unclean spirits</u> and they come out."*

Luke 4:41 *<u>Demons</u> also were coming out of many, shouting, "You are the Son of God!" But rebuking them, He would not allow them to speak, because they knew Him to be the Christ.*

Luke 6:18 *who had come to hear Him and to be healed of their diseases; and those who were troubled with <u>unclean spirits</u> were being cured.*

Luke 7:21 *At that very time He cured many people of diseases and afflictions and <u>evil spirits</u>; and He gave sight to many who were blind.*

Luke 7:33 *For John the Baptist has come eating no bread and drinking no wine, and you say, "He has a <u>demon</u>!"*

Luke 8:2 *and also some women who had been healed of <u>evil spirits</u> and sicknesses: Mary who was called Magdalene, from whom seven demons had gone out,*

Luke 8:27 *And when He came out onto the land, He was met by a man from the city who was possessed with <u>demons</u>; and who had not put on any clothing for a long time, and was not living in a house, but in the tombs.*

Luke 8:30 *And Jesus asked him, "What is your name?" And he said, " Legion"; for many <u>demons</u> had entered him.*

Luke 8:33 *And the <u>demons</u> came out of the man and entered the swine; and the herd rushed down the steep bank into the lake and was drowned.*

Luke 8:35 *The people went out to see what had happened; and they came to Jesus, and found the man from whom the <u>demons</u> had gone out, sitting down at the feet of Jesus, clothed and in his right mind; and they became frightened.*

Luke 8:36 *Those who had seen it reported to them how the man who was <u>demon</u>-possessed had been made well.*

Luke 8:38 *But the man from whom the <u>demons</u> had gone out was begging Him that he might accompany Him; but He sent him away, saying,*

Luke 9:1 *And He called the twelve together, and gave them power and authority over all the <u>demons</u> and to heal diseases.*

Luke 9:42 *While he was still approaching, the <u>demon</u> slammed him to the ground and threw him into a convulsion. But Jesus rebuked the <u>unclean spirit</u>, and healed the boy and gave him back to his father.*

Luke 9:49 *John answered and said, "Master, we saw someone casting out <u>demons</u> in Your name; and we tried to prevent him because he does not follow along with us."*

Luke 10:17 *the seventy returned with joy, saying, "Lord, even the <u>demons</u> are subject to us in Your name."*

Luke 10:20 *"Nevertheless do not rejoice in this, that the <u>spirits</u> are subject to you, but rejoice that your names are recorded in heaven."*

Luke 11:14 *And He was casting out a <u>demon</u>, and it was mute;*

when the _demon_ had gone out, the mute man spoke; and the crowds were amazed.

Luke 11:15 _But some of them said, "He casts out demons by Beelzebul, the ruler of the _demons.__ "

Luke 11:18 _If Satan also is divided against himself, how will his kingdom stand? For you say that I cast out _demons_ by Beelzebul._

Luke 11:19 _And if I by Beelzebul cast out _demons,_ by whom do your sons cast them out? So they will be your judges._

Luke 11:20 _But if I cast out _demons_ by the finger of God, then the kingdom of God has come upon you._

Luke 11:24 _When the _unclean spirit_ goes out of a man, it passes through waterless places seeking rest, and not finding any, it says, "I will return to my house from which I came."_

Luke 11:26 _Then it goes and takes along _seven other spirits_ more evil than itself, and they go in and live there; and the last state of that man becomes worse than the first._

Luke 13:32 _And He said to them, "Go and tell that fox, Behold, I cast out _demons_ and perform cures today and tomorrow, and the third day I reach My goal."_

John 7:20 _The crowd answered, "You have a _demon!_ Who seeks to kill You?"_

John 8:48 _The Jews answered and said to Him, "Do we not say rightly that You are a Samaritan and have a _demon?_ "_

John 8:49 _Jesus answered, "I do not have a _demon;_ but I honor My Father, and you dishonor Me."_

John 8:52 _The Jews said to Him, "Now we know that You have a _demon._ Abraham died, and the prophets also; and You say, if anyone keeps My word, he will never taste of death."_

John 10:20 *Many of them were saying, "He has a demon and is insane. Why do you listen to Him?"*

Acts 5:16 *Also the people from the cities in the vicinity of Jerusalem were coming together, bringing people who were sick or afflicted with unclean spirits, and they were all being healed.*

Acts 8:7 *For in the case of many who had unclean spirits, they were coming out of them shouting with a loud voice; and many who had been paralyzed and lame were healed.*

Acts 19:12 *so that handkerchiefs or aprons were even carried from his body to the sick, and the diseases left them and the evil spirits went out.*

Acts 19:13 *But also some of the Jewish exorcists, who went from place to place, attempted to name over those who had the evil spirits the name of the Lord Jesus, saying, "I adjure you by Jesus whom Paul preaches."*

1 Corinthians 10:20 *No, but I say that the things which the Gentiles sacrifice, they sacrifice to demons and not to God; and I do not want you to become sharers in demons.*

1 Corinthians 10:21 *You cannot drink the cup of the Lord and the cup of demons; you cannot partake of the table of the Lord and the table of demons.*

Ephesians 6:12 *For our struggle is not against flesh and blood, but against the rulers, against the powers, against the world forces of this darkness, against the spiritual forces of wickedness in the heavenly places.*

1 Timothy 4:1 *But the Spirit explicitly says that in later times some will fall away from the faith, paying attention to deceitful spirits and doctrines of demons,*

James 2:19 *You believe that God is one. You do well; the demons* *also believe, and shudder.*

Revelation 9:20 *The rest of mankind, who were not killed by these plagues, did not repent of the works of their hands, so as not to worship <u>demons</u>, and the idols of gold and of silver and of brass and of stone and of wood, which can neither see nor hear nor walk;*

Revelation 16:13 *And I saw coming out of the mouth of the dragon and out of the mouth of the beast and out of the mouth of the false prophet, three <u>unclean spirits</u> like frogs;*

Revelation 16:14 *for they are <u>spirits of demons</u>, performing signs, which go out to the kings of the whole world, to gather them together for the war of the great day of God, the Almighty.*

Revelation 18:2 *And he cried out with a mighty voice, saying, "Fallen, fallen is Babylon the great! She has become a dwelling place of <u>demons</u> and a prison of every <u>unclean spirit</u>, and a prison of every unclean and hateful bird."*

Appendix C

◆

Counseling Question Guide

The Official Real Deliverance Ministry
COUNSELING QUESTION GUIDE

For Spiritual Warfare and Discovering Open Doors for Demonization
Prepared by Bill Niland

This sheet will help you disclose demonic strongholds and legal rights. Permission is granted to photocopy it for personal use only.

CONTACT / PERSONAL INFO

Date _____/_____/_____

Name _____

Age _____

Phone (_____) _____--_____

Email Address _____

Referred By

_____

Church Affiliation (if any) _____

Year saved _____   Age when saved _____

PERSONAL SIN ISSUES (what are you struggling with now?)

1) _____   4) _____

2) _____   5) _____

3) _____   6) _____

EMOTIONAL PROBLEMS

Check all that apply:

☐ Depression
☐ Anger—toward whom? _____
☐ Rage—toward whom?_____
☐ Suicidal
☐ Hate—toward whom? _____
☐ MPD/DID
☐ Unforgiveness—toward whom? _____

CONFLICTS WITH PEOPLE

Y   N
☐   ☐   Do you have any conflicts in your family relationships?
         If yes, whom is the conflict with?

_____

Y   N
☐   ☐   Do you have any conflicts with another person or persons besides
         your family?
         If yes, explain:

_____

_____

EXTREME OR ABNORMAL CONDITIONS

Check all that apply:

☐ Fear	☐ Resentment	☐ Discontentment with:
☐ Self-pity	☐ Bitterness	☐ Self
☐ Envy	☐ Racism	☐ Spouse
☐ Pride	☐ Anti-Semitism	☐ Family
☐ Jealousy	☐ Unbelief	☐ Circumstances
☐ Unpredictability	☐ Doubt	☐ Other _____

☐ Self-punishment:
      ☐   Mental (describe)_____
      ☐   Physical (describe) _____
☐ Other conditions: _____

TRAUMATIC EXPERIENCES

Check all that apply:

☐ Childhood ☐ Teenage ☐ Adulthood	☐ Abortion ☐ Murder ☐ Rape ☐ Incest ☐ Molestation	☐ Sexual Abuse ☐ Emotional Abuse ☐ Controlled by Another ☐ Sudden death of a loved one ☐ Physical attack

☐ Divorce
Does it run in
your family?
  ☐ Yes
  ☐ No
	Explain checked answers (what sort of trauma, who was involved):
	
	_____
	
	_____
	
	_____	

DESTRUCTIVE HABITS
Check all that apply:

☐ Lying	☐ Lust	☐ Gluttony
☐ Blasphemy	☐ Anorexia / Bulimia	☐ Cutting
☐ Smoking	☐ Stealing	☐ Temper
☐ Drinking	☐ Constant criticism	☐ Others: _____
☐ Drugs	☐ Gossiping	_____

IMMORAL CONDITIONS
Check all that you have done or participated in:

☐ Homosexuality	☐ Adultery
☐ Lesbianism	☐ Fornication (sex while unmarried)
☐ Pornography	☐ Indecent Exposure
☐ Bi-sexuality	☐ Incest
☐ Sodomy	☐ Rape
☐ Bestiality	☐ Masturbation
☐ Others (list) _____	

Describe here:

_____

☐ I have the desires for these sorts of things listed, but have not acted upon them. List which one(s):

_____

☐ I have pictures/videos/books of the above nature. List which one(s):

_____

SOUL TIES
A soul tie is any un-Godly relationship. Examples: certain friends, family members, witches, etc. Anyone not Christ-minded.

☐ Emotional   With whom?

_____

☐ Sexual   With whom?

_____

☐ Other   With whom?

_____

OCCULT ACTIVITY – PAST OR PRESENT

1) Have you ever sought--or been subjected to as a child—HEALING, through magic conjuration and charming, such as:

   □ Removal of warts, burns, or diseases
   □ Treated by or through a spiritualist
   □ Christian science
   □ Spirit healer
   □ Psychic healing
   □ Hypnosis
   □ Metaphysical healing
   □ Any evil doctrine
   □ ս of the pendulum
   □ Divining (e.g. water witching rods, wedding ring, needle and thread, etc.---all forms)

2) Have you ever practiced: □ levitation   or   □ automatic (spirit) writing?

3) Have you ever used or worn an amulet, talisman or rabbit's foot (any good luck charms)?   □ Yes   □ No

   □ Have you ever used or worn any magic charms?

4) Have you ever had acupuncture? □ Based on 'lines' similar to the zodiac

   □ Any other sort _____

5) Have you ever been involved in Halloween trick or treating? _____

6) Have you ever been involved in martial art in any form? _____
      If so, what form? _____

7) Have you ever:
   □ practiced meditation
   □ had a spirit guide (either now or in the past)
   □ practiced mental suggestion
   □ cast a magic spell (even in fun?)
   □ practiced telepathy
   □ had E.S.P.

8) Have you ever participated in:

□ Satan worship	□ Witchcraft	□ Vampireism
□ Wicca	□ Angel worship	□ Blood drinking
□ White magic	□ A practicing medium	□ Blood spilling
□ Black magic	□ Chain letters	

9) Have you ever visited or used:
- ☐ A Psychic
- ☐ A Crystal ball gazer
- ☐ Tarot cards
- ☐ A spiritist meeting
- ☐ A Palm reader
- ☐ Tea leaves
- ☐ Yoga
- ☐ A Ouija Board
- ☐ Hypnosis
- ☐ Horoscopes
- ☐ A séance
- ☐ A Psychic Analyst
- ☐ A life / reincarnation reading
- ☐ Other _____

10) Have you had an:
- ☐ Imaginary Playmate
- ☐ or any Spirit visitors
- ☐ or Ancestors visiting

ARTICLES OR ARTIFACTS WHICH MAY BE PRESENT IN YOUR HOME

- ☐ Tarot cards
- ☐ Games of occult nature
- ☐ Good luck charms
- ☐ Mormon items
- ☐ Crystals
- ☐ Occult Jewelry
- ☐ Amulets
- ☐ Energy balls
- ☐ Occult carvings
- ☐ Masonic lodge items
- ☐ Heavy Metal or Rap music
- ☐ Occult or pagan religious objects
- ☐ Any Pagan god images (Buddha, Sun god, Egyptian, etc.)

☐ Relics or artifacts which may have been used in pagan temples and religious rites or in the practice of sorcery, magic, divination, or spiritualism.

☐ Any and **all** "Indian religion" items (dream catchers, peace pipe, anything with attached belief systems to it)

☐ Graven images of God (pictures of Jesus, Jesus on a cross, etc.)

Do you have books, comics, or videos on:
- ☐ Vampires
- ☐ The weird
- ☐ Horror

Do you read or have in your home any occult, spiritualist, or new age books such as:
- ☐ Books on astrology
- ☐ metaphysics
- ☐ Religious cults
- ☐ Black magic
- ☐ Psychic phenomena
- ☐ U.F.O.s
- ☐ Fortune telling
- ☐ Meditation
- ☐ Interpretation of dreams
- ☐ Altered states of consciousness
- ☐ Self-realization
- ☐ E.S.P.
- ☐ Mind control
- ☐ New age healing
- ☐ Clairvoyance
- ☐ Other _____

Any and **all Catholic** items (rosary, crucifix, statues, etc.)

_____

☐ Halloween items and decorations

CULTS AND RELIGIONS WITH WHICH YOU HAVE BEEN CONNECTED (Directly or indirectly)

☐ Herbert W. Armstrong   ☐ Hare Krishna   ☐ Scientology
☐ Buddhism   ☐ Zen Buddhism   ☐ Mormons
☐ Catholicism   ☐ Orthodox   ☐ Christian scientists
☐ Jehovah's Witness   ☐ Satanism   ☐ Unitarian
☐ Transcendental Meditation   ☐ Mother Earth   ☐ Witchcraft
☐ Unification Church (Moon)   ☐ Unity   ☐ Children of God
☐ Spiritual Frontiers Fellowship   ☐ The Way   ☐ The Forum
☐ Religious Research of America
☐ Metropolitan Community Church (MCC homosexual church organization)

☐ Other: _____

Have you or your family, now or in the past, been involved in:
    ☐ The Masonic Lodge   ☐ The Illuminati
    ☐ Shriners   ☐ Or any other secret society:
    ☐ Eastern Star   _____

DRUGS AND ALCOHOL ABUSE

Are you, or have you ever been, a drug user or pusher? _____

☐ LSD   ☐ Crack   ☐ Anti-depressant pills
☐ Hashish   ☐ Cocaine   ☐ Amphetamines / uppers
☐ Methedrine   ☐ Peyote   ☐ Pain killers (addiction)
☐ THC   ☐ Sleeping pills   ☐ Marijuana
☐ STP   ☐ Speed
☐ Heroin   ☐ Nembutal

☐ Or any others: _____

☐ Drinking and / or drunkardness
☐ Alcoholic

CONDEMNATION – GUILT

☐ In regard to past sins   ☐ Fear of committing sins
☐ Unforgiveness (as expressed in anger, etc.)   ☐ Unpardonable sin
☐ Fear of being unforgiven   ☐ Abortion
☐ Divorce / remarriage   ☐ Other _____
Explain checked answers here:
_____

UNGODLY TATTOOS (Skulls, demons, evil, etc.)
Describe here:
_____

Appendix C

GENERATIONAL SINS (SINS OF THE FOREFATHERS)

Many demons work legally through the generational sins. List all the sins of the forefathers and compare with sins and strongholds you checked above. What same sin(s) do you have that either of your parents have? List below:

MOM'S SIN ISSUES

_____

DAD'S SIN ISSUES

_____

GRANDPA (Mom's side)

_____

GRANDMA (Mom's side)

_____

GRANDPA (Dad's side)

_____

GRANDMA (Dad's side)

_____

GREAT-GRANDPARENTS (if known)

_____

SIBLINGS

_____

UNCLES, AUNTS, RELATIVES

_____

OTHER NOTES AND COMMENTS

_____

_____

_____

_____

_____

_____

❧ Appendix D ❧

◆

Soldier's Notes & Journal

Soldier's Notes And Journal

Soldier's Notes And Journal

Appendix Æ

◆

End Notes

End Notes

[1] James Strong, LL.D., S.T.D., *The New Strong's Exhaustive Concordance of the Bible*, (Thomas Nelson Publishers, 1996, 1996), Greek dictionary of the New Testament, 20.

[2] Mark I. Bubeck, *Preparing For Battle*, (Moody Bible Press, 1999), 106.

[3] James Strong, LL.D., S.T.D., *The New Strong's Exhaustive Concordance of the Bible*, (Thomas Nelson Publishers, 1996, 1996), Greek dictionary of the New Testament, 71.

[4] Charles C. Ryrie, *Basic Theology*, (Wheaton, IL: Victor Books, 1987), 141-142.

[5] John Maxwell, *Partners in Prayer*, (Thomas Nelson Publishers, 1996), 58.

Special Offer!

- Learn about new "Hot Topics" in the spiritual warfare arena
- Get more great teaching from Bill Niland
- Refresh yourself with stories of victory
- Keep up with all the latest ministry news

Join the Real Deliverance Ministry mailing list today

1) Just visit www.realdeliverance.com
2) Click on the newsletter icon
3) Start enjoying our E-Zine every month!

The war is real. The people are real. You are in it whether you know it or not. Don't be a war casualty. Be victorious!

If you have a testimony or something to share, we'd love to hear from you! Send it in to us, and let us know in writing if you would like it posted on our web site or not. All mail is 100% confidential. We only use material with your written permission!

E-mail it to: bill@realdeliverance.com

Or mail it to the address listed on our website at www.realdeliverance.com

Would you like to help support this ministry? Make checks payable to "Bill Niland"—or use our online secure donation system.

Printed in the United States
122507LV00004B/39/A